Lean Six Sigma

The complete guide about Lean Six Sigma
Gain benefits in your business, your job and
your life

John Rich

Copyright © 2019 John Rich

All rights reserved.

ISBN: 9781701724686

Dedication

A complete guide for Lean Six Sigma (σ) and all of its aspects, happened to get desired, accurate & efficient productivity within an organization.

This is a guide to get someone able to get acknowledgement about Lean Six Sigma's working, history, it's process cycling, strategic concepts, managements support, certifications & its levels and criticisms as well as its unpredictable benefits.

You can get almost all of the prior & beneficial information by seeking this book. We have worked hard in order to establishing this book. The main purpose of the book is to aware or to provide benefit for those who have interest in this field but have lake of resources to get valuable information about this.

All rights reserved.

Preface

The basic objective of the book "Lean Six Sigma" is to aware someone or to provide them complete knowledge about some major aspects of the industry life.

The book provides some special and common phenomenon's having some simple and common ideas to be followed to get extraordinary and profitable knowledge about information systems within some organizations.

To cover the whole information about the organizational level of information and the study of some major techniques and aspects of the existing phenomenon.

My sincere thanks to all who do value to my book and follow it by valuing my ideas and experiences. Those all, who have made me able to write something and provide my ideas to them for further life likely happenings.

It is really a great source of pleasure for me to write something, which can give my readers a complete knowledge in order to get their desired goals & requirements.

Contents

1 *"Brief History of Six Sigma"* 1
1.1 Introduction 1
1.2 Combination of Lean & Six Sigma 2
1.3 Elements of Lean Six Sigma (LSS) 2
1.3.1 Tools and Techniques 2
1.3.2 Procedures and Procedures 3
1.3.3 Mentality and Culture 3
1.4 What is Lean? 4
1.4.1 The 3 P's 5
Principles of Lean 6
1.4.1.5 Map the Value Stream 6
1.5 What is Six Sigma? 8
1.5.1 Phases 8
1.6 Relationship Between Lean & Six Sigma 10
1.6.1 Similarities 11
1.6.2 Dissimilarities 12
1.7 History of Lean Six Sigma 13
1.7.1 Eli Whitney (1798's) 14
1.7.2 Walter Chevort (PDCA Method) (1920's) 14
1.7.3 Joran and Deming (Total Quality Management) (1950's) 15
1.7.4 Easy Tuda (Lean Manufacturing) (1960's) 15

- 1.7.5 Lean 16
- 1.7.6 Six Sigma 17
- 1.7.7 Lean Six Sigma 18
- 1.8 Benefits of Lean Six Sigma 19
  - 1.8.1 Increase Loyalty 19
  - 1.8.2 Extra Efficient Results 19
  - 1.8.3 Defects removal / prevention 19
- 2 *"Process Mining & the Core Principles of Lean Six Sigma"* 20
  - 2.1 Introduction 20
  - 2.2 Process Mining 21
    - 2.2.1 Stages of Process Cycle 22
    - 2.2.2 Steps to Boost Process Cycle 23
  - 2.3 Core Lean Six Sigma Principles 28
    - 2.3.1 Focus on the Customer 28
    - 2.3.2 Understand how things really work 29
    - 2.3.3 Make your process flow smoothly 30
    - 2.3.4 Reduce waste and focus on value 30
    - 2.3.5 Prevent errors by removing variables .. 31
    - 2.3.6 Add and equip people in the process ... 31
    - 2.3.7 Perform systematic improvement activities 32
- 3 *"Comparison Between Lean & Lean Six Sigma (σ)"* 33
  - 3.1 Definitions 33

- *3.1.1 Lean* 33
- *3.1.2 Lean Six Sigma (σ)* 35
- 3.2 Core Ideas 36
  - 3.2.1 Lean 36
  - 3.2.2 Lean Six Sigma (σ) 37
- 3.3 Key Differences 37
- 4 *"Strategic concept of Lean Six Sigma"* 39
  - 4.1 Definitions 39
    - *4.1.1 Lean Six Sigma (σ)* 39
    - *4.1.2 Process* 39
    - *4.1.3 Process Improvement* 40
  - 4.2 Explanation 40
    - 4.2.1 Parts used by Lean & Six Sigma (σ) 42
    - 4.2.2 History 43
    - 4.2.3 Origin of Lean Six Sigma 44
    - 4.2.4 Wastes to be Removed 45
- 5 "DMAIC" 48
  - 5.1 Introduction 48
  - 5.2 When to use it? 49
    - 5.2.1 Main Aspects 50
  - 5.3 Steps of DMAIC 51
    - 5.3.1 Define 51
    - 5.3.2 Measure 52
    - 5.3.3 Analyze 53

- 5.3.4 Improve 54
- 5.3.5 Control 55

6 *"DMADV"* 57

- 6.1 Introduction 57
- 6.2 When is DMADV Used? 57
- 6.3 Steps of DMADV 59
  - 6.3.1 Define 59
  - 6.3.2 Measure 61
  - 6.3.3 Analyze 63
  - 6.3.4 Design 65
  - 6.3.5 Verify 66

7 *"Understanding Customer's Needs"* 68

- 7.1 Introduction 68
- 7.2 Why is it Important? 69
- 7.3 How to get understand Client's Needs? 70
- 7.4 Examples of Client's Needs 71
  - 7.4.1 High Quality 71
  - 7.4.2 Great service 72
  - 7.4.3 Prompt delivery 76
  - 7.4.4 Flexible options 77
  - 7.4.5 Durable goods 78
- 7.5 Types of Customer's Needs 80
  - 7.5.1 Proactive 80
  - 7.5.2 Reactive 81

8 "Lean Six Sigma (σ) Certification" 82
- **8.1 Introduction** 82
- **8.2 Why is it Important?** 83
- **8.3 Benefits of Six Sigma Certification** 84
  - 8.3.1 Individuals 84
  - 8.3.2 Organizational 87
- **8.4 Six Sigma Certification Levels** 89
  - 8.4.1 White Belt 89
  - 8.4.2 Yellow Belt 90
  - 8.4.3 Green Belt 91
  - 8.4.4 Black Belt 92
  - 8.4.5 Master Black Belt 93
  - 8.4.6 Champion 94

9 "Improvement Projects" 95
- **9.1 Introduction** 95
- **9.2 Key steps** 95
- **9.3 Practical Strategies** 96
  - 9.3.1 Front load the work 96
  - 9.3.2 Build a large tent 97
  - 9.3.3 Make it easy 97
  - 9.3.4 Focus on learning, not perfection 97
  - 9.3.5 Set an End date 98
- **9.4 Tips for High Quality Improvement Projects** 98
  - 9.4.1 Results vs. Accounting Focus 98

- 9.4.2 Describe your goals & objectives early & stick to them 100
- 9.4.3 Assign a frontal knowledge manager to analytics (report or application) 101
- 9.4.4 Get the end users involved in this process 101
- 9.4.5 Design to make doing things right 102
- 9.4.6 Don't under-estimate the power of one-on-one training 103
- 9.4.7 Get the Champion Involved 103
- 9.5 Why we select Improvement Projects? 104
- 9.5.1 Guidelines to select Improvement Projects 105
- 9.6 How to Identify Improved Projects? 106
- 9.6.1 Steps for Identification of Improved Projects 107

10 *"How to win Management Support?"* 110
- 10.1 Introduction 110
- 10.2 Perspectives 111
- 10.3 Priorities 111
  - 10.3.1 Increasing profit margins 112
  - 10.3.2 Reducing costs 113
  - 10.3.3 Increase the speed of delivery 113
  - 10.3.4 Improving customer satisfaction 114
- 10.4 Steps to build management support 114
  - *10.4.1 Keep the key in Sponsor's mind* 114

10.4.2	*Aware him with benefits / profits*	115
10.4.3	*Always speak the truth*	115
10.4.4	*Don't make surprises*	115
10.5	How to Win Management Support?	116
10.5.1	Steps to win:	116

11 *"Lean Six Sigma Implementation"* 123

11.1	Introduction	123
	Key Points to Implement a Project	123
11.1.1	Choose Project	124
11.1.2	Training	124
11.1.3	Team management	125
11.1.4	Make plan	125
11.1.5	Execute	125
11.1.6	Evaluate	126
11.2	Beneficial Tips	126
11.2.1	Change of behavior	127
11.2.2	Make it Compulsory	128
11.2.3	Strong Platform	128
11.2.4	Top-Down approach	129
11.2.5	High Profile Identification	129
11.2.6	Right Measurement Systems	130
11.2.7	Awareness of Cultural Differences	130
11.2.8	Having Communication Channels	131
11.2.9	Perfect to Start Lean Six Sigma	131

- 11.2.10 Communities or Forums 131
- 11.3 Steps for Successful Implementation 132
  - 11.3.1 Burning Platform 133
  - 11.3.2 Keep resources in place 134
  - 11.3.3 Teaching Methodology 134
  - 11.3.4 Prioritize activities / Tasks 135
  - 11.3.5 Ownership 135
  - 11.3.6 Right / Accurate measurements 136
  - 11.3.7 Govern Programs (Making Reviews) . 136
  - 11.3.8 Recognition with Contributions 137
- *12 "Benefits of Lean Six Sigma & Culture"* 137
  - 12.1 What Lean Six Sigma (σ) Culture? 137
    - 12.1.1 Importance of Culture 138
  - 12.2 Benefits of Lean Six Sigma Culture 139
    - 12.2.1 Increased Efficiency 140
    - 12.2.2 Better Customer Service 141
    - 12.2.3 Higher Quality Output 141
    - 12.2.4 Program Implementation 142
    - 12.2.5 A safer workplace 143
  - 12.3 Benefits of Lean Six Sigma (σ) Methodology 143
    - 12.3.1 Reduce Operational Costs 144
    - 12.3.2 Customer Complaints 146
    - 12.3.3 Improve efficiency or Timeline 146

- 12.3.4 Improve Accuracy, Controls & Policy Compliance 147
- 12.3.5 Improve Customer Service 148
- 12.3.6 Improve flow of Cash 149
- 12.3.7 Improve Regularity Compliance 149

13 *"Criticism of Lean Six Sigma (σ)"* 151

- 13.1 Why to not use it? 151
  - 13.1.1 I've never heard of a Six Sigma 152
  - 13.1.2 It's just a Fade 152
  - 13.1.3 Pretended to be Lake of time / interest 152
  - 13.1.4 Lake of Resources 153
  - 13.1.5 Showing yourself as a small-scale organization 153
  - 13.1.6 We're not a manufacturer 153
  - 13.1.7 It's is technical in calculations 154
  - 13.1.8 Cheating with Customer 154
  - 13.1.9 A poor Experience 155
  - 13.1.10 A fear of an unknown Failure 155
- 13.2 Criticisms of Lean Six Sigma (σ) 156
  - 13.2.1 Lake of Originality 156
  - 13.2.2 Inadequate / Insufficient for complex manufacturing 156
  - 13.2.3 Role of Consultants 157
  - 13.2.4 Potential Negative Effects 157

13.2.5 Over-reliance on statistics tools 157

13.2.6 Stifling creativity in a research environment 158

13.2.7 Lack of systematic documentation 159

13.3 Criticisms examples of Lean Six Sigma (σ) 159

Conclusions 161

1
"Brief History of Six Sigma"

1.1 Introduction

Lean is used to create extra efficient values for customers by minimizing waste. The Six Sigma is a technique or the phenomenon, which is used to solve problems effectively. Both Lean & Six Sigma combine to solve problems & provide best ever results to the values of customers.

Lean Six Sigma is a combination of two popular permanent improvement methods. Lean and Six Sigma. Which pave the way for operational excellence.

This is also known as a time-tested approach. It provides organizations with a clear path to achieving their missions as quickly and efficiently as possible.

Lean-Six Sigma is a process improvement process designed to eliminate problems, eliminate wastage and disadvantages, and improve working conditions to better respond to consumers' needs.

It combines Lean and Six Sigma's tools, methods and principles in a robust and powerful way to improve your organization's tasks.

1.2 Combination of Lean & Six Sigma

Lean Six Sigma provides a structured approach and collaborative toolkit to help employees build their problem solving muscles. Lean and Six Sigma are both based on scientific methodology and together support active organizations to create a problem-solving culture. This means that "finding a better way" becomes a daily habit.

1.3 Elements of Lean Six Sigma (LSS)

There are three elements of Lean Six Sigma. That are given below:

- **Tools & Techniques**
- **Procedures & Methodologies**
- **Mentality & Culture**

1.3.1 Tools and Techniques

A comprehensive set of tools and analytical techniques used to identify and solve problems.

1.3.2 Procedures and Procedures

A series of steps that manage the use of problem solving tools to ensure that the underlying causes are being investigated and that the solution is fully implemented.

1.3.3 Mentality and Culture

A way of thinking that relies on data and practice to achieve operational performance goals and achieve continuous improvement.

These three elements reinforce each other. Analytical techniques are not used effectively unless there is a process to implement them and the mentality of continuous improvement creates their need.

Improvement processes do not yield the desired results unless it includes tools and techniques that explain the activity of process steps and a culture that is based on systemic data for problem solving. Emphasize the point of view.

1.4 What is Lean?

A lean organization understands customer value and focuses on the key to maximizing it. The ultimate goal is to provide the customer with the best value through the process of producing perfect value that has zero waste.

To accomplish this, lean thinking management focuses on improving the flow of products and services, from improving technologies, assets and vertical departments to leveraging entire value streams horizontally across technologies, Assets, and departments reach consumers.

Eliminating waste with full cost streams instead of isolated locations compared to traditional business systems creates processes that require less effort to create products and services at a human cost, less space, less capital, and lower costs.

General Chat Lounge Companies respond to changing consumer desires with high quality, high quality, low cost and fast delivery times. Plus, information management gets easier and more accurate.

1.4.1 The 3 P's

There are 3 P's of Lean. Which are generally categorized as:

- **Purpose**
- **Process**
- **People**

1.4.1.1 Purpose

What customer issues will the customer solve to achieve his goal of business development and prosperity?

1.4.1.2 Process

How will the organization examine the stream of critical value to make sure that every step is valuable, accessible, available, appropriate, flexible, and that all stages are connected to flow, drag and drop.

1.4.1.3 People

How can the organization ensure that everyone is responsible for making a consistent assessment of this important flow in terms of business purpose and lean action in each important process?

How can each person touching the value stream be proactive in running it properly and permanently improving it?

Principles of Lean

There are five major principles on which a Lean relies. The principles are given below:

- **Define the Value**
- **Map the Value Stream**
- **Set Pull**
- **Create Flow**
- **Seek Continuous Improvement**

1.4.1.4 Define the Value

The customer describes the value of a product or service. Therefore, the first step is to identify consumers. Ask yourself, what is the importance of the customer?

Find consumer expectations for your product or service. Classify the activity into non-value added, value added and unblocking value added.

1.4.1.5 Map the Value Stream

Value stream mapping shows the stages of the workflow process for a product or service. Value stream mapping helps identify and eliminate NVA activity.

This in turn helps you reduce the delay in the process and thus improve the quality of the product or service.

1.4.1.6 Set Pull

Set the bridge view by meeting the system beat time. Bat time is the rate at which a product must be ready to meet consumer demand.

JIT (just in time) is a tool to develop the bridge tool system. This ensures a smooth workflow without interruption. It also helps reduce inventory levels.

1.4.1.7 Create Flow

Make the customer flow by ensuring a consistent flow system in product or service development. Flow will improve the process to maximize process efficiency.

1.4.1.8 Seek Continuous Improvement

Finally, you must make continuous efforts to improve the existing business processes to meet the changing customer needs. This allows for elimination of rubbish and ensures free product and quality service defects to consumers.

1.5 What is Six Sigma?

The Six Sigma approach focuses on identifying and eliminating anything that could cause a change in process. When the variables are removed, the process results can be predicted accurately each time.

By designing the system so that these clearly predicted results fall into the acceptable performance zone from the customer's point of view, this process eliminates errors.

But the engineers at Motorola went a step further. They knew from experience that many process changes were not effective because they could not find the true cause of the problem. Also, the changes they have made will not be sustainable, as operators shift over time to work in a real way.

1.5.1 Phases

To solve some specific problems within organizations, Six Sigma was organized with five steps.

1.5.1.1 Define

The stages of this process analysis are set out in this stage and the expectations or desired performance for this process are defined from the customer's perspective.

This is to ensure that change does not disappoint the customer experience, but rather enhances it.

1.5.1.2 Measurements

At this stage, the current performance of the process, product or service is evaluated to determine what's really going on, especially from the customer's perspective.

This is to ensure that the analysis and solution is based on actual performance, not on theoretical or strategic information.

1.5.1.3 Analyze

At this stage, the process, product or service is analyzed to determine the sources and sources of the variables that cause this problem using the measured data.

This is to ensure that the original symbol is identified, not just a symbol.

1.5.1.4 Improve

At this stage potential changes are made to the process, product or service, and a solution set of changes is designed and evaluated.

This is to ensure that the solution produces the desired effect and that the variability is reduced or eliminated.

1.5.1.5 Control

Changes are implemented at this stage, support systems are also updated and processes, products or services are controlled. Generally, statistical process control to ensure that the solution is fully implemented in a sustainable manner and to indicate that the performance or not.

1.6   Relationship Between Lean & Six Sigma

Lean & six sigma are inter-mixed because they are different, they are complementary.

Similarities allow them to connect well together. Differences ensure that analytics tools and solution options are available that will improve the process, product or service.

This is because of the similarity that both types of analysis can occur at the same process, product or service simultaneously.

1.6.1 Similarities

The similarities of Lean & Six Sigma are as follow:

1.6.1.1 Customer's Experience

Both rely on the definition of value that is based on customer experience. The customer is the king or queen.

1.6.1.2 Improvement Projects

Both are implemented using improvement projects that will typically be implemented by a small cross-functional team.

The duration of the project and the size of the team will depend on the scope and scale of the process in which the product is being evaluated for improvement, the scope and scale of the process, product or service.

1.6.1.3 Manufacturing Operations

Both have migrated beyond manufacturing operations and are now used for all functions and for all processes encountered internally and externally. They are also used in all industries, including industrial, consumer, government, education, and non-profit.

1.6.1.4 Statistics Based

Both rely on statistics to determine current performance and to determine the impact of future performance.

Data collected in the Lean Sigma Project can often be used to support both Lean Analysis and Six Sigma Analysis. Relying on data helps ensure that the true root cause is identified.

1.6.2 Dissimilarities

There are some dissimilarities also rely as well as some similarities between Lean & Six Sigma.

Dissimilarities are as follow:

1.6.2.1 Differ in focus

Various focuses to identify the problem. Focuses on lean waste & Saks Sigma focuses on variability, at any deviation from target performance.

1.6.2.2 Variety of Techniques

They use different variety of techniques. Six Sigma uses statistical techniques to analyze and create solutions that are supported by data visualization.

This leads to the myth that lean is easier than sexy sigma, because it is easier to understand about lean, while many people are afraid of numerical analysis of sexy sigma. The fact is that both types of analytics are easy to perform with today's statistical support tools.

1.6.2.3 Document solutions

Document Different types of documents for solution. The lean solution has been documented with a revised value stream map that causes work flow changes and changes to work instructions often over many stages of the process.

The Six Sigma solution is documented with a control plan to monitor setup changes and process changes and respond to changes. It will also affect work instructions and change the measurement approach or system frequently.

1.7 History of Lean Six Sigma

The foundation of Lean Six Sigma was developed in 1780's after that there were become more developments & it further reach to the required or the final term of "Lean Six Sigma".

Lean started with Toyota in the 40's and the Six Sigma debuted at Motorola in the 80's. Although they have been taught as separate methods for many years, it is blurred and it has now become commonplace to combine the two Lean and Six Sigma teachings to cultivate the best of both worlds.

1.7.1 Eli Whitney (1798's)

During this revolution, the standard revolution began and was led by Eli Whitney.

It developed the concept of interchangeable parts that greatly improved the uniformity of finished products during mass production.

These interchangeable parts enable even the most skilled workers to produce final products at a fast and low cost.

1.7.2 Walter Chevort (PDCA Method) (1920's)

It was during this period that the concept of control of statistical processes was developed. This approach enabled better planning and implementation of mass production processes.

Schwartz also developed a PDCA methodology that includes

- Planning (exploring what needs to change and how to do it)
- Doing (making changes and testing changes)
- Processing

That the change produced the expected result is acting or ensuring that change becomes part of the production process.

1.7.3 Joran and Deming (Total Quality Management) (1950's)

Important influences came from Joseph Jurran and Edwards Deming during this period. Both of these figures incorporate total quality management (TQM).

Which included the human aspect as an important part of quality management at Total Quality Management (TQM) & the use of statistical quality control methods to improve the manufacturing process. Has contributed immensely to this idea.

1.7.4 Easy Tuda (Lean Manufacturing) (1960's)

This period saw significant contribution from the Japanese in the quality management movement. Eji Tuda, the founder of Toyota and Toyota Production System (TPS), developed the concept of eliminating all the garbage in production to ensure that the production process was as efficient as possible.

This TPS performance-driven approach led to the development of the Just in Time Principle, which stated that the parts needed in the entire production process were acquired when needed. This was done to reduce inventory overcrowding.

The TPS approach developed by Edge Toyota is what is now known as Lean Manufacturing. Lean manufacturing is now widely used in many companies all over the world.

1.7.5 Lean

Lean started with Toyota in the 40's and the Six Sigma debuted at Motorola in the 80's. Although they have been taught as separate methods for many years.

It is blurred and it has now become common to see both Lean and Six Sigma teachings combined for the best cultivation in the world.

When the lean is mentioned, it is usually associated with Toyota and Taichi Ohno. It originated as the Toyota Production System (TPS) and over the years has evolved into a comprehensive system for both the manufacturing and service sectors.

Pressure is too much about improving flow, reducing waste, and maximizing profits. The methodology behind Lean is about solving process flows and wasting issues. This is essential to increase production capacity.

It is very important to understand both the approach and the accompanying toolkits when solving problems.

It doesn't matter as long as a tool works lean or six sigma comes from. Combining these methods is the perfect shot to put you in the right mindset, tactics and tools to solve your problem.

1.7.6 Six Sigma

In the business world, product variations exist on one curve. The concept of this 'common' curve was established by Carl Frederick Gauss in the 18th century. As a standard of measurement for product variations, the Six Sigma is of the 1920s. It was only after that that Walter Chevert identified three Sigma as a point where a process needed improvement.

As a name, the "Six Sigma" was thought of by Motorola engineer Bill Smith. In the mid of 1980s, Motorola's chairman, Bob Galvin, along with his own team of engineers.

They developed the "Six Sigma" measurement system. It was not only a measure of productivity, but also a cultural change in the company.

Six Sigma helped Motorola realize powerful bottom-up results at their company, and efforts saved 16 billion dollars. Since the success of the Six Sigma in Motorola in the 1980s, it has been adopted by countless companies around the world. In each case, it has proven to be a successful way of doing business and is widely praised by US leaders.

1.7.7 Lean Six Sigma

When the two are put together, Lennox Sigma becomes an effective business management system that improves quality, reduces waste and maximizes profits.

This is done by developing the necessary processes and tools that easily open the door to business performance and success in each area.

Lean and Six Sigma are integral to the development of quality management in businesses and companies around the world.

1.8 Benefits of Lean Six Sigma

Organizations face increasing costs and new challenges every day. Lean Six Sigma offers competitive advantage in the following ways.

1.8.1 Increase Loyalty

Smooth process results in better user experience and increased loyalty.

1.8.2 Extra Efficient Results

Identifying more efficient process flows leads to higher bottom-line results.

1.8.3 Defects removal / prevention

Replacing reduces costs and removes waste to prevent defect detection.

1.8.3.1 Agility

Standardizing the process has the potential to drive organizational "agility" and everyday challenges.

1.8.3.2 Profitability

Reducing lead times increases efficiency and profitability

1.8.3.3 Employee Development

Employee involvement in efforts improves morale and accelerates people's development.

2
"Process Mining & the Core Principles of Lean Six Sigma"

2.1 Introduction

Six Sigma has been one of the most successful management philosophy in the last 20 years. However, the current challenges facing companies, such as the growing process and complexity of the supply chain, as well as high volumes of unstructured data, cannot easily be overcome by relying on traditional Cisco Sigma tools.

To meet this need based on design science, we offer a vision to integrate Process Mining into the Six Sigma tool set to improve data analytics. The results of the first specialist assessment workshop provide insights into its applicability and ideas for future research.

2.2 Process Mining

Process mining is an automated, systematic way of defining an 'as is' phase of BPI to identify current workflows or process waste, obstacles, disagreements, and opportunities.

Processing relies on validated data from the mining IT system and replaces manual process mapping, which is inherently humane and time-consuming.

In addition, process mining is used as a fast, accurate method throughout the BPI life cycle to repeat process analysis to maintain and monitor process changes

Processing mining frequently appears in a PPI initiative as changes take effect, and the process requires constant monitoring and evaluation. Once the mining process is set up it can be easily "switched on" to re-evaluate the refining process and create a clear measurement standard at any stage.

Process mining takes practicality that even well-documented and controlled processes generally do not conform to the plan and requires objective verification to improve them.

2.2.1 Stages of Process Cycle

Using fact-based data, not subjectivity, processing mining builds trust and certainty in the early stages of BPI. It helps a lot in the improvement of business process & all its circumstances.

There are 4 stages or phases by which a Process Mining helps to improves business process or to work for the betterment of Business Process Improvement (BPI):

- Accurate Data Based Analysis
- Measureable Results
- Process Focus

- Results Oriented

2.2.2 Steps to Boost Process Cycle

It also boosts the Process Cycle of Lean Six Sigma. It can boost the DMAIC structure or the cycle of Six Sigma. Which can be underdone by 5 steps & used to provide accurate, desired & best efficient results having extraordinary yields.

As, we have already read that DMAIC is the combination of 5 steps. These 5 steps are as follow:

- Define
- Measure
- Analyze
- Improve
- Control

Process Mining is being used in almost all Business Project Improvement Cycles. Because it helps you to be more efficient in every step of the DMAIC cycle. Let there are 2 indicators or parameters known as "X" & "Y". With the help of these, we can easily understand the functioning or the processing of Data Mining Boosting.

2.2.2.1 Define

In the explicit phase of the DMAIC cycle, we primarily define the issue we are going to consider. We need to know what the business problem really is and what are the concrete issues we are trying to solve.

Based on the general understanding of the problem that this project is targeting, we determine its breadth and estimated timelines and resources. Processing mining gives you a process model (all the activities and paths between them), and it gives you instantaneous insight into how the various process activities are related and the stages of the process.

Too many stats about frequency and duration. What's more: Process mining immediately reaches a level where there are obstacles and lumps in the process.

So it is clear that in the first step, where you look for the truth, and explain what the problem is that needs to be solved, the process is the ability to discover and quickly identify the obstacles and obstacles.

2.2.2.2 Measure

Measuring is a data collection step in which we translate customer needs into indicators of an excellent performance process that will be measured over a period of time.

This process output indicator (also known as "Y") tells us how well the process performs from the client's point of view and how well their needs are met.

The performance metric baselines from the measurement phase will be compared to the performance metric at the end of the project to determine if a significant improvement has been made.

Good data is at the center of the DMAIC process, and to identify the gap between current and desired performance, we need to collect high quality data on process performance.

The ability to process stats in processing mining tools like Disco enables us to be more accurate when we compile process Y.

2.2.2.3 Analyze

In the analysis phase, we try to identify, verify, and select the root cause of the problem so that we can eliminate it. A number of potential causes are identified through various techniques such as root cause analysis and process mapping and further analysis is preferred.

Data is analyzed to understand the magnitude of the contribution of each of the main causes, "X" in the process performance metric, using "p" values alongside histograms, Pareto charts and line plots, with "Y".

Process Mining provides the analyst with an unmatched level of required process maps. Process maps are automatically generated by the Process Mining software and depend on the process stored by the software used to support the business process, many different about this process.

2.2.2.4 Improve

In the improvement phase we begin to address the problem. We're going to look for a possible solution to our problem and then we're going to put it into practice and test it.

This is the part that goes to the creative minds. Often using brainstorming techniques, we try to find creative solutions to fix process problems and prevent relapse.

Improving the process should be a very rewarding activity. The point is, improvements don't always look as good as we would like them to. This is where the Perth-based mining experts have come to help the lean Sigma team.

Not only do we make improvements visible through processing mining, we also make them measurable. You see the effect of the change that was implemented in front of your eyes.

2.2.2.5 Control

The purpose of this initiative is to maintain the benefits. Monitor improvements to ensure continued and sustainable success.

- Create a control plan.
- Update documents.

We recommend creating books that will help you continue to monitor the process and analyze trends on a regular basis. If the book shows a deficiency in the process, plan a response to monitor each of the steps.

2.3 Core Lean Six Sigma Principles

Some features of Lean & Six Sigma combine to form some core principles. There are 7 major principles of Lean Six Sigma (σ).

- Focus on the Customer
- Understand how things really work
- Make your process flow smoothly
- Reduce waste and focus on value
- Prevent errors by removing variables
- Add and equip people in the process
- Perform systematic improvement activities

2.3.1 Focus on the Customer

CTQ is a system technique used to normalize or measure the quality of any work or process. It describes the elements of your service or offer that they consider to be critical of the quality.

In writing such as making sure they are measurable, CTQs provide the basis for determining action steps that help you understand how well you perform against these important requirements.

It is important to focus on the customer and the value add value. Because typically only 10-15% of process steps add value and often only 1% of the total time of the process is represented.

These statistics can be surprising, but they should get your attention and help you understand potential trash in your organization. When you improve your performance in meeting the CTQ, you also have the potential to win and retain more business and increase your market share.

2.3.2 Understand how things really work

The value stream describes all stages of your process - for example, from customer order to product execution or payment to delivery of services.

By drawing a value stream map, you can uncover the non-value-added stages of waste and these areas and ensure that this process focuses on meeting CTQs and increasing value.

Value stream shows all of the functions that create value and create value, your product or service concept and launch your customer order through the supply chain.

These value creation and non-value creation processes include the process by which information from the customer can be processed and the product has to be transformed in the customer's way.

2.3.3 Make your process flow smoothly

This concept provides an example of different thinking. If possible, use single piece flow, moving away from batches, or at least reducing the size of the batch.

Either way, identify the non-value-added steps in the process and try to remove them - make sure they don't delay the steps to increase value.

The concept of pulling, not pushing, connects us with understanding the process and improving flow. And this can be an important factor in avoiding obstacles. Excessive production or moving things too quickly is useless.

2.3.4 Reduce waste and focus on value

Doing so is another important factor in improving flow and efficiency. Generally, there are 8 types of waste.

Through this process performance can be greatly improved. Some strips that have no side effect on the performance output are discarded. Of course, if you can stop the waste in the first place.

2.3.5 Prevent errors by removing variables

Managing reality, using accurate data, helps you avoid jumping to conclusions and solutions. You need the facts! And that means measuring the right things correctly.

Data collection is a process and needs to be managed accordingly. The use of control charts enables you to interpret data accurately and understand variations in the process. Then you know when to take action and when not to.

2.3.6 Add and equip people in the process

You need to get people involved in the process, equip them for both feel and be able to challenge and improve their process and how they work.

Involving people is what organizations need to do if they want to be truly effective, but, like many Lean Six Sigma principles, if that is to happen, it requires different thinking.

2.3.7 Perform systematic improvement activities

Six Sigma's DMAC works here. Which are Definition, Measurement, Analysis, Improvement and Control.

Sometimes the purpose of criticism is that sometimes the stand-alone 'lean' goal is that improvement is not done in a systematic and standard way.

In Six Sigma, DMAIC is used to improve the existing process, but this framework is lean and, of course, equally applicable to Linux Sigma. Where a new process needs to be developed, the DMADV of Design for Six Sigma (DFSS) method has been used.

3
"Comparison Between Lean & Lean Six Sigma (σ)"

3.1 Definitions

3.1.1 Lean

"Lean is defined as the term, the process or the method which is used to remove wastes from a specific or existing process to increase productivity."

In lean, any activity that does not add value to the product or service end user needs to be removed. Here are eight key areas to look for in lean waste:

- Errors in a process
- Overproduction
- Waiting or idle time between operations
- Unused Skills
- Waste transport methods
- Additional inventory
- Unnecessary actions by employees or machines
- Additional processing, or measures that do not add value

The enemy of lean manufacturing is waste. Waste is defined as an activity that consumes resources without adding value.

Waste can take the form of unnecessary transportation, waste inventory, or wasted movement, but it all works to make the production process less efficient and more prone to produce poor results.

Lean focuses on the big picture and seeks to eliminate waste not only at isolated locations, but also at full value. Lean is not just about improving quality.

It aims to create an organizational culture for sustainable improvement, empowering employees, and eliminating waste.

3.1.2 Lean Six Sigma (σ)

"Lean Six Sigma is a combination of two popular permanent improvement methods. Lean and Six Sigma. Which pave the way for operational excellence".

Basically, people who use Lean Six Sigma try to eliminate waste in the ways described by Lean while also keeping **DMAIC** & **DMADV** in place.

- **DMAIC** (Define, Measure, Analyze, Improve, Control)
- **DMADV** (Define, Measure, Analyze, Design, Verify)

Combined, these two approaches help companies become more efficient at all tasks, while also creating better quality products and services.

As its name implies, Six Sigma and Lean Quality Improvement Factors combine to produce Rogue Sigma. Supporters of quality improvement quickly realized that they could solve many problems by creating a quality improvement hybrid that works best in both worlds.

In practice, Lean uses lean methods and tools to detect and remove sigma loss. Lean Six Sigma also employs the **DMAIC** cycle from Sigma to eliminate garbage in the process. And it is the combination of "Define, Measure, Analyze, Improve & Control."

3.2 Core Ideas

The main idea on which Lean & Lean Six Sigma rely, are as follow.

3.2.1 Lean

- One way to eliminate trash in system production is known as lean.
- Its main theme or function is to remove waste.
- Its focus is to flow of processes.
- Uniformity in process production
- It's Based on visuals
- Improving production by increasing process efficiency.

3.2.2 Lean Six Sigma (σ)

- Lean Six Sigma is the approach used to perform better tasks by systematic methods
- Its main theme is to provide accurate results as client's requirements
- Its focus is to produce extra efficient yield
- Its aim is production
- It's Based on statistical methods

3.3 Key Differences

Lean & Lean Six Sigma (σ) interrelate with one another. They are also variate from each other in many circumstances. The major or key differences between Lean & Lean Six Sigma (σ) are as follow:

1. Lean is defined as a systematic way of blushing waste from the existing processes while Lean Six Sigma is the technique of working with some scientific or systematic methods to provide accurate & desired results.
2. The main concept of the Lean is to remove waste while Lean Six Sigma has to eliminate it with the removal of variations.

3. The Lean was manufactured or developed by Toyota in 1940's onwards while the first concept of Lean Six Sigma was given in 2001's.
4. Lean is a flow focused process while the Lean Six Sigma focuses on statistical & systematic methods of yield efficiency. It's also defined as problem focused technique or methodology.
5. The tools used in Lean are based on visuals while the tools used in Lean Six Sigma Are Mathematical or Statistical.
6. Implementation of Lean results as uniformity while results generated by Lean Six Sigma are related to flow time of operations.
7. The aim of Lean is to increase productivity by the removal of wastes while the main aim of Lean Six Sigma is to use both methodologies (i.e. Lean & Lean Six Sigma) to fulfill the requirements of client & make him satisfy.

4
"Strategic concept of Lean Six Sigma"

4.1 Definitions

Some important definitions regarding Lean & Lean Six Sigma are as followed:

4.1.1 Lean Six Sigma (σ)

As, we know that It is the combination of Lean & Six Sigma. So it is also defined as the best problem solving methods to help organizations to achieve their mission, goal & satisfaction of their customers.

4.1.2 Process

Implementation is a series of processes that involves building a product or providing a service. Everything we do is a process.

For example, pairing your shoes, making a cake, treating a cancer patient, or producing a cellphone.

4.1.3 Process Improvement

Improvement in the process requires employees to better understand the current state of how it is implemented so as to remove barriers to customer service.

Since every product or service is the result of a process, acquiring the skills needed to eliminate waste, rework or inefficiency is essential for an organization's growth.

4.2 Explanation

Employees are hired based on their expertise in a particular field. Baker is good at baking and surgeons are good at performing surgery.

Professionals are experts in working on a process, but they do not necessarily have to be skilled at working on a process.

Learning to work and improve processes requires continuous improvement experience and education. This is where Lean Six Sigma comes from.

Lean Six Sigma Lean and Six Sigma is a compatible management concept. Lean is traditionally focused on the elimination of eight types of waste / mold classified as Defects, Overproduction, Awaiting, Unused Skills, Transportation, Inventory, Movement, & Additional processing.

Six Sigma (σ) seeks to improve the quality of process results by identifying the causes of errors (manufacturing and business) and reducing process variability.

In harmony, Lean aims to achieve a consistent flow by strengthening the links between process stages, while Six Sigma focuses on reducing process variability (in all its forms) for the steps of this process. And thus enables those connections to be tightened.

Lean Six Sigma Manufactures Lean and Six Sigma to reduce production costs, improve quality, speed up, stay competitive and save money. With Six Sigma, they get less change in parts.

Lean focuses on saving money for the company by focusing on the types of waste for the company and how to reduce the waste.

4.2.1 Parts used by Lean & Six Sigma (σ)

The both terms, Lean & Six Sigma have improved each other to create a balanced and systematic solution to save money and create consistently better parts. The parts are as follow:

- Cason
- Value Stream Mapping
- 5S System
- Logan
- Error Proofing (Poca U)
- Production Maintenance
- Set Time Reduction
- Reduce Lot Size
- Line Balance
- Schedule Leveling
- Standard Work
- Visual Management
- Identify
- Define
- Measure
- Analyze
- Refine

- Control
- Standardize
- Integrate

4.2.2 History

Motorola unveiled Lennox Sigma in the United States in 1986 to compete with the Cousins business model in Japan.

In the 1990s, Allied Signal hired Larry Busdy and introduced Six Sigma in heavy manufacturing. General Electric's Jack Welch consulted with Baddy and introduced Six Sigma to General Electric.

Six Sigma counterfeiters from Saks Sigma to Delhi during the 2000s. In 1989, these standards were expanded to include certification for individuals in all professions and professions.

The first concept of Lean Six Sigma was developed in 2001. In the early 2000's, the six principles of Sigma were expanded to other sectors of the economy, such as healthcare, finance & supply chain etc.

4.2.3 Origin of Lean Six Sigma

Lean started with Toyota in the 40's and the Six Sigma debuted at Motorola in the 80's. Although they have been taught as separate methods for many years, it is blurred and it has now become common to see both Lean and Six Sigma teachings combined for the best cultivation in the world.

It is very important to understand both the approach and the accompanying tool kits when solving problems. It doesn't matter as long as a tool works.

Combining these methods is the perfect shot to put you in the right mindset, tactics and tools to solve your problem.

There are two ways at a glance:

- ***Lean uses PDCA***
    - Planning
    - Do
    - Check
    - Act / Adjust

- ***Six Sigma (σ) uses DMAIC***

- Define
- Measurements
- Analyze
- Improve
- Control

4.2.4 Wastes to be Removed

Lean & Six Sigma is combined for the improvement of production within an organization by eliminating wastes. The wastes are also terminated as "**D.O.W.N.T.I.M.E**". These wastes are of 8 kinds, which are given below:

- Defects
- Over-production
- Waiting
- Non-utilized skills / talent
- Transportation
- Inventory
- Motion
- Extra-processing

4.2.4.1 Defects

When some pieces have to be thrown out or reworked because they are not inside the tolerance. These are called defect waste or equipment waste.

Products or services that are out of specification that require resources to fix.

4.2.4.2 Over-production

Giving too much product before a product is ready for sale is called over-production.

Overproduction means producing more results or outputs than a recorded or appropriate quantity.

4.2.4.3 Waiting

Wasting time or waiting to deliberately waste time. It refers to the time spent waiting for a product to be created. It can be terminated as Waiting for the final step of the process to complete.

4.2.4.4 Non-utilized skills / talent

This happens when an individual is disqualified for an assigned job. In this case it does not work properly.

Because this thing goes beyond his wishes and he is not able to fulfill all that he has been assigned.

In the result, they are not effectively engaged in the process or set of processes.

4.2.4.5 Transportation

Loss of supply or waste of transport is the loss or waste that is wasted on the time of delivery of the goods to the recipient. In this term, the transport of goods or information that does not need to be carried out from one place to another refers to be transportation waste.

4.2.4.6 Inventory

When spending time loose that doesn't make money or Inventory or information that is sitting idle. Waste disposal is also known as extra processing waste, and waste in processes is also known as motion waste. This is called inventory waste.

4.2.4.7 Motion

People, information or goods create unnecessary activity because of the workplace.

4.2.4.8 Extra-processing

Extra-processing is about Performing an activity that is not required to develop working products or services.

5
"DMAIC"

5.1 Introduction

The process is the focal point of DMAIC. The method seeks to improve the quality of a product or service by focusing not on the output but on the process that created the output. The idea is that focusing on the process leads to more efficient and permanent solutions.

DMAIC is the problem-solving methodology of Lean Six Sigma. It consists of five Phases. That are Define, Measure, Analyze, Improve and Control.

DMAIC is often considered to be the main block of the Six Sigma method. By using it, businesses can begin to improve without the unnecessary experience.

"Measurement is the first step that leads to control and eventually to improvement. If you can't measure something, you can't understand it. If you

can't understand it, you can't control it. If you can't control it, you can't improve it."

(H. James Harrington)

DMAIC is a data driven improvement cycle that can be implemented in the business process to detect defects or inaccuracies, especially. The goal of employing DMAIC is to improve, improve or strengthen the existing process.

The development of the DMAC approach goes to Motorola, but it is largely a further extension of Toyota's built-in system.

5.2 When to use it?

Some organizations initially add an additional step to the DMAIC, called Identity, where they evaluate whether the DMAIC is the right tool to use for their needs.

DMAIC uses a project team that is trying to improve an existing process. DMAIC provides structure because each step of the process consists of tasks and tools that help the team find the final solution.

Although DMAIC can be configurable, it is not strictly linear. This process encourages project teams to step back from the previous steps if more information is needed.

It is used in most of the organizations, when they faced some difficulty in producing the required results for the needs of their clients. This 5 steps technique is used to get more & desirable results at the time of deficiency.

5.2.1 Main Aspects

There are three important things to consider when assessing a situation for which the DMAIC will be used:

- There is a clear problem of some form with the current process or set of processes.
- Has the ability to reduce variables such as lead time or defects while improving variables such as cost savings or productivity.
- The situation is quantifiable. The process itself involves measuring data and the results can be reasonably explained by the appropriate amount.

5.3 Steps of DMAIC

DMAIC is the abbreviation of 5 terms. Which are direct to a set of processes. That processes are utilized to remove wastes as well as the improvement of results for client's satisfaction.

Following are five steps that can be taken to achieve the best and most desirable results:

- Define
- Measure
- Analyze
- Improve
- Control

5.3.1 Define

In this phase, you have to ask yourself two very important questions in the definition phase.

- What is the problem?
- How has the issue affected my company?

Once you have the answers to these two questions, you can begin to define the goals of your project. You can then create your available resources, support, and a plan.

The tools to use during this phase are a project charter or workflow diagram. The project begins with creating a team charter to identify team members, select a process that will improve the team and clearly define the purpose of the project.

The project team will then identify the CCTQ to measure its impact on users. This step is completed when the team prepares a process map that includes the process information and output.

5.3.2 Measure

This phase involves planning and implementing data collection that provides reliable and important data. The data shows how the process is performing and how the Six Sigma narrative helping to identify the villain in the transformation.

From this point forward, the project team's efforts are focused on reducing or minimizing variations as much as possible.

During the measurement phase, you need to take a closer look at the pre-existing systems so that you can see what's working and what's not working.

Once you've measured all the data, you can determine the root of the problem and start looking for ways to solve it. Data collection is a helpful tool during this phase.

Includes core business process performance.

- Plan a data collection for this process
- Collect data from multiple sources to determine the type defects and measurements
- Compare the results of the customer survey to determine the reduction

5.3.3 Analyze

Once the process performance is determined, the analysis phase can help identify potential causes of the problem. A sub-process map can help identify problems that may arise.

And tools like ANOVA and regression analysis can help narrow these issues down to the root causes. At this stage, the team is able to quantify the financial benefits of solving this problem.

- Determine the reasons behind the systematic delay
- Explain the "right" way of doing things
- Determine whether the process is running to the maximum extent possible

- Determine whether the process should be improved or re-engineered

In the analysis phase, you need to analyze your results from the measurement phase. By analyzing the data, you can reduce the main cause of loss and error.

5.3.4 Improve

Once the root cause of the problem is revealed, the correction step is focused on finding a permanent solution to the problem.

This is where the creativity of the project team comes into play, which seeks the answer to a long process problem.

The team then tests a proposed solution in a pilot program to test whether the solution is effective and financially viable.

During this phase, you can look for possible solutions, test and implement these solutions, and make any necessary changes.

Improve the target process by developing creative solutions to problem solving and prevention.

- Create innovative solutions using technology and discipline
- Develop and plan implementation plans

5.3.5 Control

At this stage, the project team documents the new solution that it has developed so that it can be transferred to the implementation owners.

The project team then executes the solution according to the timeline and key milestones they have developed. Once the solution is implemented, the project team monitors it for several months and hands it to the process owner if it meets performance expectations.

Your work has just begun when you implement a new process. The time has come to maintain this process. This final phase of DMAIC involves making lasting improvements and supporting strategies that will maintain the effectiveness of your process.

Businesses can implement many positive changes using DMAIC, but these changes will only occur if employees work to improve them permanently.

It is helpful to create a control plan and clearly define the roles and responsibilities of each person who will assist in maintaining this process.

- Control the improvements that helps to keep the process on the new course
- Stop going back to the "old way"
- Ongoing monitoring projects need development, documentation and implementation.

6
"DMADV"

6.1 Introduction

"DMADV is a Six Sigma framework focused primarily on the development of a new service, product or process that is contrary to already existing improvements.

Measuring, Analyzing, Designing, Validating are especially useful when new strategies and measures are put into practice because of its basis in data, early identification of success, and thorough analysis.

6.2 When is DMADV Used?

DMAIC is used, when the problem you want to solve is for a process that already exists but does not meet the expected level of performance.

DMAIC is used when you want to correct an existing process that does not meet expectations.

Alternatively, DMADV is used when you want to design a new process, which should meet the required level of performance from the beginning.

DMADV can also be used when an existing product or process needs to be redesigned rather than permanently fixed. The spirit of DMADV lies in understanding customer needs and CTQs that are most often expressed.

It is a Six Sigma standard method used to design a new process with the purpose of delivering the final process to the client correctly. The goal of the DMADV process is to create a high quality product, which fully meets the needs of the user and the user during each stage of the project.

Each letter of the acronym DMADV is one of the five key steps in a project improvement initiative: determine, measure, analyze, design and validate.

6.3 Steps of DMADV

The purpose of some Sigma procedures is to minimize errors in a product line by looking at all processes that assist in the completion and delivery of a product or service.

Improving the effectiveness of these methods and quitting waste tasks are ways to make the entire manufacturing process more efficient. This leads to shorter lead times, improved gross margins, and more reliable production lines.

The word "DMADV" is actually an abbreviation of 5 words. These words are actually 5 major steps to work with the improved production of an organization. The 5 steps are as follow:

- Define
- Measure
- Analyze
- Design
- Validate

6.3.1 Define

"This phase consists of defining the problem, defining the customer set, identifying the goals, and outlining the target process."

DMADV is about identifying the purpose, process or service of the project in this first phase of the process. Not only from the organization's point of view, but also from the perspective of other stakeholders, including consumers.

It should clearly explain what guidelines are important for product or service development, and if there is a potential risk and schedule of production.

6.3.1.1 Goals

The goals of the first phase are to identify the purpose of the project, process or service, and to identify realistic and measurable goals displayed from the organizational and stakeholder perspectives, and then develop schedules and guidelines for them.

To review and identify and evaluate potential risks. During this move a clear definition of the project has been established, and every strategy and target should be in line with the expectations of the company and consumers.

6.3.1.2 Results

Project leaders want and identify their needs, which they consider to be of paramount importance to consumers. Identify wants and needs through historical information, customer feedback, and other information sources.

- Teams were gathered to execute this process
- The metrics and other tests are aligned with customer information

6.3.2 Measure

"This step involves deciding which parameters need to be quantified, working on the best way to measure them, collecting the necessary data, and performing the measurements through experience."

The purpose of this stage of the DMADV process is to collect and record data that relates to the CTQ measures identified during the first phase.

The data that is collected during the measurement phase is essential to this process, as it will be used to run the rest of the process.

In the case of DMADV, there is no CTQ yet in the measurement phase. However, there is no new product yet, skip the production process.

During this measurement phase, it is about determining what a customer thinks about new thinking. These factors are later linked to quality, leading to CTQ.

6.3.2.1 Goals

Measure quality, or factors that are important to CTQs. The steps to be taken should include:

- Defining Requirements
- Identifying critical design parameters
- Setting up Scorecards
- Risk Assessment
- Production Processes

Evaluate the potential of the product and the capacity of the product. Once the value of these factors is known, then an effective method can be taken to begin the production process.

Which metrics are essential to the stakeholder and it is important here to translate customer needs into clear project goals.

6.3.2.2 Results

The second part of this process is to use the default matrix for data collection and record the specifications in such a way that it can be used to help run the rest of the process.

All processes required to successfully develop a product or service have been assigned a matrix for subsequent evaluation.

6.3.3 Analyze

"Identification of performance goals and the possibility that inputs influence the execution of results are considered in this section."

The analysis of these DMADV processes is closely linked to the measurement phase, as the project team will analyze and evaluate all data collected.

As a result, improvements can be made during the production process. During this analysis phase, design alternatives are developed and the maximum set of requirements is met.

During this phase, the total lifetime cost of the design is also estimated. After the detection of various design alternatives, a somewhat artificial design is developed (functional details) that meets the default CTQ maximum.

6.3.3.1 Goals

The steps that will be taken during this phase will include:

- Designing Alternatives
- Identifying the optimal combination of requirements
- Designing conceptual designs
- Reviewing them
- Selecting the best components
- Choosing
- Creating the best design

It is during this phase that the total cost of the design is estimated.

6.3.3.2 Results

The result of the manufacturing process is tested by internal teams to create a baseline for improvement.

Teams arrange the final process in place and make adjustments as needed.

6.3.4 Design

"Work on the details, refining methods if necessary and planning design validation come at this stage."

The design stage of the DMADV process consists of the design of products or services that are perfectly tailored to the customer's needs.

During this phase, the project team uses the data from the previous steps, creating a product that suits the customer with all possible additional adjustments that may be needed.

This is a detailed and high quality design that will be made into a prototype. During the preparation of this prototype, they also observe the production process.

The purpose is not just to produce a production process that produces good products, but also one that is logistically efficient.

6.3.4.1 Goals

This phase of DMADV includes both a detailed and a high level design for the selected alternatives. The design elements are preferred and from there a high level of design is developed.

Once this step is completed, a more detailed model will be prototyped to detect the possibility of errors and make necessary corrections.

6.3.4.2 Results

The results of the internal test are compared with the customer's wishes and needs. Any additional adjustment is required.

Improved manufacturing processes are tested and customer feedback groups provide feedback before the final product or service is widely released.

6.3.5 Verify

"Examining the design to make sure it is tailored to the plan, ensuring process trials are in place so they work and starting production or sales falls into this category."

The verification process of the DMADV process may be the last step, but this is not the end of the process. In order to protect the quality, it is important to continue with product validation and adjustment.

In this final step, the design is final and the product is ready to be sold. During this phase, the project team reviews the user and user experiences, and will make the necessary adjustments to better meet customer needs.

The project team will also determine additional CTQ measures to monitor consumer feedback after the final product is delivered.

6.3.5.1 Goals

In the final step, the team verifies that the design is acceptable to all stakeholders. Will design be effective in the real world? Several quality pilots and production runs will be necessary to ensure the highest quality possible.

Expectations will be confirmed here, deployments will be enhanced and lessons learned will be documented. The certified step is to move the product or service into operation as usual and to make sure the change is sustainable.

6.3.5.2 Results

The final step in the procedure is continuous. When a product or service is being released and customer reviews are coming in, this process can be adjusted.

The matrix is further developed to track customer feedback on the product or service.

New data can bring other changes that need attention, so early adoption may lead to new DMADV applications in later areas.

7
"Understanding Customer's Needs"

7.1 Introduction

Your users have some needs. And you may already know what those requirements are already. But each of them has specific needs. Finding out what your customer needs and requirements.

The process used to point out customer's needs (either external or internal) or feedback in order to provide the best in class service or product quality is called "Understanding the customer's need". This process is active and stable to meet the changing needs of consumers over time.

Many companies think that they know what their clients want. Very few people spend time investigating and verifying.

We don't want to guess at the Six Sigma DMAC process, we want to be sure. To do this we reach out to our customers, clients, partners and suppliers to make sure we are listening to what's really important to them.

7.2 Why is it Important?

The better you deliver against customer needs, the higher the customer satisfaction. Many satisfied customers are loyal and can even help promote your products and services.

Many people fall into the trap of understanding their user based on their experience. To truly understand you, you need to constantly ask and explain. The wants and needs of your customer's change.

If you do not know what your customer wants, how can you possibly know that you can be delivered if you are expecting? Which indicates an inappropriate and inappropriate action. This can hurt customer trust and help them find other ways to benefit from your company.

We want the voice of the client to follow the principles of permanent improvement. For example, you may want to improve your post-purchase experience so that your company can increase sales by turning customers into loyalty loops instead of a less robust active research loop.

7.3 How to get understand Client's Needs?

Data is collected later in the DMIC measurement phase. However, what we want to achieve is consumer expectations, as they describe it in their own words.

When a customer is doing something to you, he or she is asking a lot of questions inside. In fact, she couldn't say it all directly because it could have hit her.

As he is constantly asking himself, will you provide him with good quality results? This thing can definitely hurt you. So the best way to do this is to tell them about your services. And make sure the customer is completely satisfied with you.

7.4 Examples of Client's Needs

Some specific questions, a customer wants to know are categorized in some specific examples. There may be some examples.

- High Quality
- Great service
- Prompt delivery
- Flexible options
- Durable goods

7.4.1 High Quality

High quality is a feature that everyone demands. A customer's top priority is to work with the most unique and high quality. The results presented to the customer's basic needs are to be standardized. Which is a worthy cause.

Standardization of any product greatly increases its value. The quality and uniqueness of a product or result on a business and industrial level affords a certain degree of quality. So this process is very important, but very important, for customer approval or satisfaction.

7.4.2 Great service

The interesting thing about the service is that it includes both concrete and unobtrusive aspects. For example, the physical aspects of an airline are the availability of seats, departure frequency, lounge quality, etc., while the unaffordable aspect is staff friendliness and courtesy matters.

Office cleaning is quite solid and can be done. Reasonably measured, but the effectiveness of the rehabilitation program is more difficult to measure, especially in a new facility. The unavoidable element of the service means that it cannot be stocked and difficult to measure reasonably.

- Some characteristics of Service
- The service is relatively unreliable
- The service is designed and used at the same time
- Is involved in the creation and delivery of customer service
- Leadership and management skills are very different from manufacturing

7.4.2.1 Some tips for Excellent Service

Excellent customer service creates life-long loyal customers who want to send your business to friends, family and colleagues.

Providing this kind of excellent customer service starts with a genuine desire to please our customers, but you have to think beyond selling your product or service.

When visiting your store or website, what you think and feel and what you can do to improve it, you need to consider the overall experience of your customers.

There are 7 major & most important tips for managing great services. Those are given below:

- Know your product or service
- Be Respectful
- Be Responsive
- Say Thank You
- Listen
- Train your Staff
- Ask for Feed back

7.4.2.1.1 Know your product or service

To provide you with good customer service, you need to know what you are selling inside and out.

Be aware of the most common questions consumers ask and know how to describe the answers that will satisfy them.

7.4.2.1.2 Be respectful

Customer service can often involve emotions, so it is important to make sure that you and the other people you handle your customer service are always courteous and respectful.

Never let your emotions come to the forefront of your customer's desire to be happy.

7.4.2.1.3 Be responsive

There is nothing worse than the irresponsibility of a customer trying to get help, resolve a problem, or find out more about what you are selling.

It is important to respond promptly to all inquiries, even if just to say that you are seeing this issue and will be in touch again. Some answers are always better than none so that the user is not ignored.

7.4.2.1.4 Say Thank you

Thanksgiving is memorable, and it reminds your customers why they purchased your store or hired your company.

Regardless of what type of business you have, saying thank you after every transaction is one of the easiest ways to start a good customer service habit.

7.4.2.1.5 Listen

Listening is the easiest secret of customer service. This means what your customers are saying out loud and they are having a non-verbal conversation.

Keep an eye on the symptoms that they are angry about, while listening to what they say directly to you.

7.4.2.1.6 Train your staff

It is important to make sure that all of your employees, not just your customer service representatives, understand the way they interact, interact, and otherwise support customers.

Provide staff training that provides your staff with the tools they need to deliver good service through the entire customer experience.

7.4.2.1.7 Ask for feedback

You might be surprised when you ask them what they think of your business, products and services.

You can use customer surveys, feedback forms, and questionnaires, but you can also make it a common practice for users to ask for feedback first when you are completing your orders.

7.4.3 Prompt delivery

Instant or Prompt Delivery is the heartfelt desire of every customer. Everybody wants to place an order today and get their delivery tomorrow. In this category he expects too much. If such an expectation is fulfilled, then it becomes the great source of pleasure for him.

Therefore, it is an essential process to meet customer expectation and facilitate prompt delivery. Doing so increases the customer's trust in you and your organization, and he / she is definitely satisfied with your services.

7.4.4 Flexible options

Flexible options are about some relaxations or some favorable things to do or provide to customer.

Flexible Options Trading Flexibility and facilities are trading in the following options more than ever.

7.4.4.1 Contract flexibility

The terms of the contract such as the expiration date, strike price, and settlement type can be specified according to your strategy requirements.

For example, you can trade contracts as the expiration date is the end of the month, and the final contract is a cash settlement based on closing prices.

7.4.4.2 Commercial flexibility

Agreements can be prepared and implemented on the same day. You don't have to wait until tomorrow.

7.4.4.3 Margin offsetting

Margin offsetting is allowed with other future and option contracts.

7.4.4.4 Alternative to OTC options

OSC listed / trade flexible options offer solutions to issues related to OTC options, such as counterparty risk and various rules that are subject to the OTC transaction.

7.4.5 Durable goods

Durable goods are a category of consumer products that do not need to be purchased often because they last a long time. Usually lasts for three years or longer.

They are also known as enduring or enduring users. Durable goods are expensive goods that last for three years or more. Businesses and consumers buy big-ticket items only when they feel confident about the economy.

When they are unsure, they stop buying durable goods until things get better.

7.4.5.1 Key Points

Some Key Points for Durable Goods are as follow:

- Sustainable goods are key economic indicators that measure new orders placed with domestic manufacturers to supply factory hard goods in the near future or in the future.

- Higher numbers of durable goods indicate the economy, while a lower number indicate a downward trend.
- Strong durable goods order numbers can cause a rally in the bond market while a weak number can lead to a decline.

7.4.5.2 How it works?

Consumer goods is often divided into two types:

- Durable
- Non-durable

Sustainable products have a long extension and usually do not hurt or consume when you use them. Since they are made in the last days, durable goods are often more expensive than non-durable goods, which often have to be bought in the short run.

7.5 Types of Customer's Needs

Customer's inner voice or hidden requirements can be of two types. These types are given below:

- Proactive
- Reactive

7.5.1 Proactive

It is better to be dynamic rather than reactive in life. The same principal applies when submitting to a Voice of Client.

In the active model you are reaching out to people even before a problem or task is completed. Here are some ideas:

- Use mockups and beta versions to experiment with volunteers before moving into production
- Send surveys to a potential customer's base
- Model Office are most useful for this purpose. They are known as Duplicate versions. Duplicate is a great way to get advanced data.
- Interview customers and partners on how they see your process. Just ask their opinion.

7.5.2 Reactive

Just because an activator is preferred over a reaction does not mean that the reactive source has no value. In some cases, it can be very easy to collect reaction data.

Your organization probably has large stores of reaction data. Here are examples:

- Online Feed back
- Customer Service Logs
- Make some Reviews

7.5.2.1 Online Feed Back

You can always send surveys only after performing or selling the service.

7.5.2.2 Customer Service Logs

You may have comments on your website or a letter to the editor. There are review sites and social media comments.

If you've built an iPhone app, iTunes has a wealth of user feedback. Restaurants can take advantage of Yelp.

7.5.2.3 *Make some Reviews*

If people are returning a product or calling for help, you can easily quantify this data and make it public to find common issues.

8
"Lean Six Sigma (σ) Certification"

8.1 Introduction

A set of tools and techniques used by companies to improve production processes, eliminate defects, and guarantee quality is known as "Six Sigma (σ)". Six Sigma certification helps professionals who are skilled at identifying and removing risks, mistakes, or defects in a business process.

Six Sigma is a toolkit in which many business leaders work in manufacturing and project management to improve all aspects of their business processes. The Six Sigma process aims to reduce the rate of errors in the development and preparation process, creating a baseline for ongoing quality, improvement and consistency.

8.2 Why is it Important?

Learning the six sigma ways can help affect your career. The ability to add Six Sigma certification to your resume proves your commitment to improve your business skills, analytics skills and work output.

Companies invest in Six Sigma certification because it offers a designer set of tools and techniques that help improve the process within an organization.

The main goal of the certificate is to validate those who have the skills needed to identify and eliminate errors in a process. Professionals who receive the Six Sigma certification become key stakeholders in improving the quality of work in their organizations.

They try to bridge the gap in manufacturing and business processes by applying standard processes and establishing measurements that minimize the possibility of defects.

8.3 Benefits of Six Sigma Certification

Six Sigma Certification proves beneficial for everyone. It can be profitable for:

(a) Individuals / Employees
(b) Organizations

8.3.1 Individuals

The benefits of Six Sigma Certification for individuals are as follow:

8.3.1.1 Help to reduce Risks & eliminate Defects

The acquisition of six sigma certification and project management software such as CELOXIS enables an individual to be critical of an organization's ability to detect and eliminate errors.

8.3.1.2 Improve Business & Quality improvement

After you take our six sigma courses, you will be able to analyze a company's manufacturing and business processes and take steps to improve them.

You will also be able to fully review the current methodology and understand how they affect quality performance.

Moreover, the certification shows that you can achieve the level of quality improvement that organizations need, making sure to closely monitor the monitoring process, which means straying from the path. Be it, there is not much deviation.

8.3.1.3 You will become valuable for every industry

Certified people at Six Sigma are aware of dozens of different ways that can be used to streamline business processes, improve employee acceptance, reduce costs, and increase revenue.

8.3.1.4 Ensure Compliance

Sigma demands very high quality requirements. Because of this, a significant number of vendors, buyers and guardian organizations apply Sigma's six standards when testing products or accounts.

Six Sigma certification professionals can help their organizations maintain profitable contracts and comply with international standards.

8.3.1.5 Rise to Managerial Positions

Once you have completed your Six Sigma course and obtained your certificate, you will have a clear idea of how to measure and quantify the financial benefits of performing any of the Six Sigma projects.

Sigma's six certifications help professionals gain risk assessment and financial management skills. Such expertise is highly appreciated by senior and middle level management for senior management positions.

8.3.1.6 Excellent Salary

Becoming a Six Sigma Certified is no small feat. Study included. Passing exams is not easy. In addition, moving from one belt level to the next requires real work for years.

So it is not surprising that six Sigma certification professionals are well paid.

8.3.1.7 Get hands-on experience in Quality Management (QM)

The Six Sigma training process involves working on industry plans and applying theoretical principles to real-life scenarios.

Starting a Six Sigma course helps you gain complimentary experience before joining the workforce.

8.3.2 Organizational

Six Sigma Certification can also prove beneficial for Organizations as well as individuals. The main benefits are as follow:

8.3.2.1 Improved productivity

It provides extra efficient quality & makes beneficial results for an organization. It helps to improve quality & productivity of any organization in a profitable manner.

8.3.2.2 Reduced Costs

Defective reductions reduce waste, so lower production costs and higher profits. Failure to create a standard product can be expensive. Creating a non-standard product or service can significantly reduce its cost.

8.3.2.3 Boosts customer's confidence in your business

Implementing Six Sigma helps to improve or increase the self-confidence or the trust in your organization. It helps customers to get through their orders to you.

This thing helps a lot to make an organization or any kind of industry unique about its production.

8.3.2.4 Get Reputation & Stakeholder's Trust

Consumers and stakeholders rely on a company whose employees have the relevant qualifications. If a significant number of your employees are Six Sigma Certified, that means their first priority will be quality.

A company that operates with quality is competitive and thus builds trust among investors and partners.

8.3.2.5 Reduce employee trade and training costs

As stated in a post on Research Gate, the DRIC methodology can also be applied to HR management.

8.4 Six Sigma Certification Levels

Six Sigma professionals are present at every level - each one has a different role to play. Although the implementation and roles of Six Sigma may vary, a basic guide here guides who does what.

Many well-known organizations today combine the Six Sigma standardization methods with lean manufacturing methods, eliminating the need to make their organizations as efficient as possible. These are the sigma belts and certification levels you can get:

- White Belt
- Yellow Belt
- Green Belt
- Black Belt
- Master Black Belt

8.4.1 White Belt

The White Belt certification provides evidence of the basic level of knowledge for the six Sigma's core concepts. Professionals are considered the Six Sigma White Belt if they do not receive regular certification programs or extended training.

In a session with Lean Six Sigma related methods and word reviews, workers at all levels of an organization are shown how they contribute to effective, reliable results. With this basic premise, the White Belts participate in projects and problem solving tasks related to quality management and waste reduction.

Understands the Six Sigma concepts from an awareness standpoint. The goal of the White Belt is to understand the basic concepts of Six Sigma.

8.4.2 Yellow Belt

The Yellow Belt Certificate indicates that you have learned how Six Sigma works, how its articles apply to the workplace, and how to focus your time when you learn the process.

The yellow belt designation marks the emergence of six sigma concepts that go beyond the basic principles provided for the white belt. The Yellow Belts may have attended training sessions within a day or two, and promoted the information that should be assigned to a project in collaboration with the desired team members.

They can guide limited scope projects and help managers at the higher belt level. It participates as a member of a project team. Review project improvement process improvements. Yellow Belt is where the fun of just starting to eliminate defects within the enterprise system.

8.4.3 Green Belt

The Green Belt Certification focuses on advanced analysis and resolution of problems related to quality improvement projects. The Six Sigma guides and manages the Green Belts projects, supporting the Black Belt.

Green belt training is valuable to individuals in roles such as project management, healthcare management or financial management, which will give them an understanding of performance measurement and tools such as control charts and failure modes and effects analysis (FMEA).

After the certification, professionals are ready to take charge of the projects by establishing links between Lean Six Sigma concepts and their organization's goals.

They can put leadership tools into practice, find opportunities to eliminate trash, and gain useful statistical insights. Leads Green Belt projects or teams. The average salary for green belts starts at 75,000$.

8.4.4 Black Belt

Black belt certification indicates that you are an expert on Six Sigma philosophy and principles. Black belts are known as change agents in an organization that lead project teams.

This advanced training requires prior knowledge of LSS strategies as professionals specialize in the skills they need to plan, guide and plan more sophisticated and comprehensive projects or organizational changes.

Need to be explained. Students at the Black Belt level course gain a solid understanding of how to drive changes to the organization, analyze statistics, deploy lean principles, and oversee plans for the Green Belts team. Throughout the Black Belt level course, professionals demonstrate what they have learned and learned through a project for their employer or a nonprofit organization. This leads to problem solving projects, Trains and coaches project teams. On average, Black Belt companies save about $ 230,000 per project. Average salary estimate for a black belt. 88,000 per year.

8.4.5 Master Black Belt

A master black belt represents the lean sigma success structure. He has extensive experience and is a leader in his field. A strong black belt with strong leadership and problem solving skills can become a master black belt in Lean Six Sigma.

This position indicates that a specialist takes a broad view of the strategy throughout the business, and integrates teams. It trains & coaches the Black Belts and Green Belts.

By developing key metrics and strategic direction, Six Sigma does more at the program level. The average salary for a master black belt starts at 132,000$ & can exceed 200,000$ annually.

8.4.6 Champion

The first level of Six Sigma certification is called a Champion. Champion is not a belt, but it is an important function of a Six Sigma project or organization. The champion's primary role is to ensure that the operational plans are in line with the strategic level business objectives.

A champion is a high level manager who guides the LSS strategy and deployment. Based on the goals set by the Executive Leadership, the champions ensure that all measures are taken together to meet the development needs of a company to reduce waste and eliminate defects.

With the help of the Master Black Belt, these managers mentor the leaders involved in the implementation of the LSS and observe their progress.

They translate the company's vision, mission, goals and measure to create organizational deployment plans and identify individual projects. Identify resources and remove road blocks.

9
"Improvement Projects"

9.1 Introduction

In terms of "process improvement plans", plans can be defined as temporary or short-term efforts designed to improve the process and, in turn, improve the performance of key business indicators. However, what business leaders worry about is improving results.

9.2 Key steps

However, here are five key steps that, when implemented correctly, can greatly increase the difficulty of a smoothly executed process improvement plan that results in success:

1) Building stakeholder relationships
2) Establishing sound ground rules
3) Using appropriate facilitation skills

4) Incorporating improvement procedures within the project
5) using the powerful testing procedures within each project

9.3 Practical Strategies

There are 5 practical strategies of the management of successful improvement projects, are given below:

- Front load the work
- Build a large tent
- Make it easy
- Focus on learning, not perfection
- Set an End date

9.3.1 Front load the work

It's important to take time into planning, collect baseline data, develop measurement plans, and make mistakes in managing your team.

One point he shared is that at the beginning of the reform plan, your calendar has to be time-consuming to focus on the task ahead. Springer promised that saving time in the early stages of work saves time later.

9.3.2 Build a large tent

This includes how a team leader can avoid doing all the work. It shared a matrix tool (pictured below) to help teams identify the key people in their organization who want to stop, let it happen, help it or make it work. Have the ability to ensure success.

9.3.3 Make it easy

Because team members are often involved in the improvement of full-time jobs, successful teams must take full advantage of existing structures to operate. Adding improvements to the scheduled meetings is a beneficial thing to do.

9.3.4 Focus on learning, not perfection

Many teams spend time trying to meet their goals, steps, and test of change before embarking on a project. Instead, they should be flexible in the project as the team learns.

"Everything should be in pencil. So, Focus on learning, not on chopping."

9.3.5 Set an End date

Improvement projects have hardly any natural consequence. "There is still a lot to do!" However, to keep up with the pace of improvement, setting a deadline compels you to keep track of your goal.

Work backwards to plan when specific activities need to be taken to reach important milestones.

9.4 Tips for High Quality Improvement Projects

Tips are the most important directions which are used to direct someone to some specific places or to do something special in order to get perfect results. There are 7 useful tips for the high quality of the improved projects:

9.4.1 Results vs. Accounting Focus

Most results improvement project teams operate under one of two principles: accountability measurement or improvement measures.

Projects that measure accountability primarily focus on components or punishments based on whether individuals are following certain processes and procedures.

An excellent example would be to pay a furniture bonus (or receive a fine) based on compliance with certain medical measures at a facility. The speed at which people measure attention is shifted to whether a particular data point is right for a particular person or not.

When this happens, people are concerned about the negative light and the resulting punishment. With this approach, there is no rising wave that lifts all the boats.

Certainly, some people at the bottom may be better, but personal interest takes priority rather than examining the process and focusing on interventions that will help advance the overall goal. Improvement in results is delayed or never reaches its full potential. However, it is important to test whether your project demands it or if it should focus on measuring for improvement instead.

9.4.2 Describe your goals & objectives early & stick to them

In order to move the project forward, the project team must specify a smart:

- Specific
- Measurable
- Feasible
- Relevant
- Timeframe

Explaining this in the first or second workgroup meetings is usually the best time. Setting these parameters gives everyone an opportunity to work on the efforts that will return the best bang for the buck.

This task is made clear when the work is moving to the side track and therefore not profitable. Purpose statements are a great tool for project managers to promote discussion and more.

Without them, projects become bloated, less agile, and end up throwing away rather than delivering value quickly. This project is not a crime against resilience.

Purpose statements, and even goals, can change shape as data is excavated, but as a guideline, on a goal and two to four goal statements for the initial scope of a project. It's better to focus.

- Focused on the results
- Contains specific acquisition goals and consistent goals
- Add a timeline
- Define the target population clearly
- Are harmonious
- Provide prices

9.4.3 Assign a frontal knowledge manager to analytics (report or application)

This process requires a manager or interviewer who is fully aware of it and is well aware and aware of all aspects.

This is a very important step as almost all systems depend on it.

9.4.4 Get the end users involved in this process

End users need to be involved in this process. Successful outcome improvement teams cannot be just executives or individuals who are not on the frontline.

When choosing end-users to attend, it is important to think about the long term. Which customers trust the rest of the staff? Which Consumer Improvement Plan Can Succeed? Often these people are very busy.

Successful projects select these individuals to participate and help them schedule their schedules so as to adopt a plan to repeat requests and improve outcomes.

Amazing projects get support in their purchase before kicking off the project. Lastly, a comprehensive mindset builds in which you build the built-in super user and champion.

9.4.5 Design to make doing things right

First, analytics tools should be simple and easy to use. Remove barriers to access to information needed to improve. Otherwise, creating work boundaries is costly to facilitate this process.

The second design element incorporates interventions that are included in the workflow to facilitate the right task. Interventions that require more work (for example, needing hand wash documents each time the caregiver enters the room) often fail. The load is great.

If clinicians need to order three new orders (eg, a flu shot, a lab, and a script) that require five extra minutes with the patient, this is an intervention that will not succeed, unless serious.

9.4.6 Don't under-estimate the power of one-on-one training

Improvement of results occurs only when analytics and interventions are adopted. These champions and super users need to become subject matter experts, those who know the process well, those who rely on others, and who Better early adopters. Wherever possible, train super-users and major champions one-on-one for 20 minutes on analytics tools.

9.4.7 Get the Champion Involved

No other feature of a highly successful outcome improvement plan is to compensate for a project that has lost a leader who is a subject matter expert and who has purchased it.

The champion needs to convey the "why" of the project to the group and ensure that the reasons are echoed by those involved at all levels.

The best champions intrinsically inspire the workgroup and others to work towards a common goal. This is what forces everyone to solve the problem and make improvements. The champion regularly shares the vision.

9.5 Why we select Improvement Projects?

Choosing the right plan can have a big impact on your business. If done properly, the processes will run more efficiently in 3-6 months, employees will feel satisfied and happy to improve the business and eventually the stakeholders will see the benefits.

If the project is selected illegally, a project can be selected that does not include the entire business, project barriers cannot be removed due to other business priorities, the team may feel ineffective and The end result may be less than ideal.

No one wins in this situation, especially the quality manager who can find the same people the next time they need to.

9.5.1 Guidelines to select Improvement Projects

Here are five guidelines, which are followed to get succeed in order to select Improvement Projects.

1) Ask your business leader for the three biggest business problems. Make sure your project is one of those issues or is directly related. This will ensure that your management team is paying close attention to the project and removing road blocks immediately.

2) What are the three biggest problems your users look at? View customer complaints logs, call center telephony and call customers who have discontinued your company service. Create a Pareto chart to prioritize matters. This will help in prioritizing the project and choosing the plan.

3) Is the project manageable? Can this project actually be completed by a team within six months? If in the long run, you may lose members moving to other jobs or the team may

be frustrated that they are not making a difference.

4) Will this team have a measurable impact on the business process or financial bottom line? Do not start a project without knowing what will benefit the business. This will keep your team motivated along the way.

5) What is your ability to process? If you aren't measuring your process, how do you know it needs improvement? Make sure you know the extent to which this process is currently generating errors and explain the desired results for your project.

9.6 How to Identify Improved Projects?

When improvement plans are properly aligned with an organization's strategy, they help achieve business goals. Often, however, it can be a challenge for organizations to choose the most appropriate improvement plan from the pool of many potential projects.

To address this issue, this research proposes a new approach designed specifically to maintain value generated in other ways, but to identify rigorous, objective projects, and prioritize or select. Reduces the time or effort required for.

Special guidance was received for the organization where this example was presented, on which improvement plans should go forward. In addition, this example provides direct evidence of the rigor and flexibility of the proposed approach, whereby other organizations can learn to improve the project and take advantage of it.

9.6.1 Steps for Identification of Improved Projects

When developing a future state, it is important to define a key objective for the process that will guide the design. For staffing, the goal may be to fill a position in less than two months.

For the pharmaceutical filing process, the goal may be to recruit as many as possible. A clearly defined business objective for the process provides the design driven vision.

9.6.1.1 Understand the real constraint

When preparing for the future state, it is important to understand the constraints of the actual process of the present state and to assess to what extent these obstacles will remain in the future.

For example, developing pharmaceuticals requires the time needed to validate new equipment for future state development. A typical future map describes the state of action 12 or 18 months from now.

If a new piece of equipment is in place and takes 30 months to verify, the existing equipment becomes an obstacle to a future state map. Some constraints are real while others are just assumed.

9.6.1.2 Focus on Projects, that help to achieve the goal

When analyzing the distances between current and future states, one should focus only on projects that will help achieve the overall goal. In many cases, the improvement plan is full of projects that have no clear connection to the overall purpose.

Most companies have only limited resources. The resources available should therefore be focused on projects that really need to be done.

9.6.1.3 Define the Options

In almost every instance, there are several different paths to achieving the future and the overall purpose of the process. For example, when focusing on capacity building in a bottleneck machine, this goal can be achieved by reducing cycle time, unplanned timeouts, changing times or process production.

Defining alternative "project packages" is helpful for understanding business plans and making smart resource allocation decisions.

9.6.1.4 Merge / Integrate existing steps into the plan

Plans and plans planned for the future and the future need to be integrated into the overall plan to the extent that they affect the future. However, one needs to be careful and review whether the delivery of these measures is realistic.

For example, a company that was mapping out its manufacturing process identified two projects that were expected to significantly reduce the process time. However, when the team reviewed these plans, it became clear that the expectations for the impact were unrealistic.

9.6.1.5 Be creative and adapt to the situation

Value stream mapping is usually focused on a product family. However, in many cases the concept of the product family is limited. In many industries, goods are not dedicated to a particular product or family, and the processing paths may vary from run to run.

Similar problems arise in many service processes. For example, when users can choose between different channels (Internet, Phone, Email, etc.)

Focusing less on a product family doesn't really provide much insight into the available improvement opportunities. In such cases, the value stream approach can be enhanced by combining mapping with other tools such as broken analysis.

10
"How to win Management Support?"

10.1 Introduction

"Administrative or Management support is defined as the management's consent to promote business practices. It is also being terminated as (MS)."

Including championing new ideas and providing resources that people need to take business initiatives.

10.2 Perspectives

First, a project manager and his sponsor look at the project in a completely different way. Those of us in project management are all about cost, schedules and quality. We need to pay attention to the details. Executives don't really care about the details unless there is a mistake.

Their approach is about control and stability. They want to assure that the project is in control and cause as little disruption to stakeholder groups as possible.

10.3 Priorities

From a sponsorship standpoint, a successful project will deliver better operational performance in the future and allow it to work even better to achieve these goals:

- Increasing profit margins

- Reducing costs
- Increase the speed of delivery
- Improving customer satisfaction

10.3.1 Increasing profit margins

Profit margin is the profitability of a product, service, or business. This is expressed in percentages. The higher the number, the more profitable the business. There are two types of Profit Margins.

- Gross Profit Margin
- Net Profit Margin

10.3.1.1 Gross profit margin

Gross profit margin is usually applied to a specific product or line rather than the entire business. Calculating gross profit margin helps the company determine pricing decisions, as lower profits may mean that the company needs to charge more to make the sale of a particular product worthwhile.

10.3.1.2 Net profit margin

In contrast to gross profit margin, net profit margin is a calculation that reflects the profitability of an entire company, not just a product or service.

The percentage is also one percent. The higher the number, the more profitable the company will be.

Low profit margins can indicate a problem that may interfere with profitability, which involves unnecessarily high costs, productivity issues, or administrative issues.

10.3.2 Reducing costs

Cost reduction is a process that companies use to reduce your costs and increase your profits. Depending on the services or products of a company, the strategy may vary. A customer is most satisfied when it comes to good quality at reasonable cost.

So this process is very important to make your production better and more dynamic. A company that provides more services at a reasonable price. Of course its market value and customer trust will be even better.

10.3.3 Increase the speed of delivery

Delivery speed is a process in which the customer is provided with his required delivery as soon as possible.

The best and fastest delivery a company or organization can offer its customers. The more their customers' trust will be restored.

10.3.4 Improving customer satisfaction

After delivering, customer satisfaction is most important thing to make sure. It is probably a mandatory thing.

Customer satisfaction is a commonly used term in marketing. This is a measure of whether a company's product or service meets or exceeds customer expectations.

10.4 Steps to build management support

There are some practical steps a project manager can take to get executive support.

- Keep the key in Sponsor's mind
- Aware him with benefits / profits
- Always speak the truth
- Don't make surprises

10.4.1 Keep the key in Sponsor's mind

Operational efficiency, a supervised project, and a sense of stability within stakeholder groups. If sponsors feel that a project is out of control, they will begin to bridge the gap between themselves and the project.

10.4.2 Aware him with benefits / profits

Inform your sponsor of progress in delivering operational benefits, and in this context focus only on budget and schedule.

10.4.3 Always speak the truth

Never play the game of project managers, in which they do not tell the sponsor about any problems and say that everything will work out.

Always inform your sponsor of any important issues, and come up with your own plans to tackle those issues. This approach will build a trusting relationship between you and your sponsor, and give your sponsor confidence in you and your team.

10.4.4 Don't make surprises

Never let your sponsor be in for a surprise. It has to do with the political environment.

There is nothing worse for a sponsor than the surprise of another executive who says something like, "My people are telling me that there is a problem with your project."

10.5 How to Win Management Support?

There are some individuals who can effectively and successfully mobilize their teams. In essence, you cannot be a successful manager unless you can lead the team. They need to be fully engaged, committed, and satisfied in order for organizations to thrive and achieve their potential.

Employees need to buy into the mission, culture and values of their organization, appreciate the value of their role, and be prepared to do what they are told.

10.5.1 Steps to win:

There are 10 major steps or techniques. By following them, you can win the management support:

- Show your Abilities
- Become a personality
- Become collaborative

- Make decisions
- Arrive Early, stay Late
- Be careful
- Present well
- Tackle with problems
- Assist with Development
- Provide Occasional Treatment

10.5.1.1 Show your abilities

Employees are more likely to respect you as a manager if you are technically strong, have good skills, and have proven themselves in your chosen field.

If they are having trouble with a particular client, project, or work, this is great if you can step in and help. If you are not capable of doing what is assigned to your team members of equal or higher quality, you will never really have full authority.

10.5.1.2 Become a personality

There will be some distance between you and the general workforce, but with that you should be able to engage with staff on a personal level.

Allow employees to see who you are as a person, beyond the context of a professional, and tell them that your game has more than just barking instructions. You need to be employed as a person, in different teams and departments.

10.5.1.3 Become collaborative

Employees rarely respond well to power-hungry leaders. So, as long as possible, be open, accessible and cooperative. If one of your staff members has a good idea of how a system or process can be improved, consider it appropriate.

This change can make things easier for everyone and help your team achieve its goals. You should seek input from employees on many issues. This does not mean they get the final say, but it does help them voice their opinion and influence your decision.

10.5.1.4 Make decisions

To become a successful manager, you need to have courage in your beliefs. If you sit on the fence the whole time, it won't be long before employees begin to make their decisions and begin to feel overwhelmed by your authority.

But there is no point in taking practical steps. You have to do your research, consult your staff and then make wise, consistent decisions that will stand the test. If you make mistakes and change your mind, it is not necessary to have a problem.

It is better to stick to this method than what is not working. But you can't afford to back down too often, because it makes people question your decision.

10.5.1.5 Arrive early, stay late

Always try to guide by example. You do not want all your employees to be at their desks when they are already at work, nor do you want to move home while they are still working.

As a manager, you need to show that everyone is together. One for all and one for all. If you want to climb the career ladder and be part of the leadership and management team, maybe longer time is essential. But at the same time, it's sometimes your job to bridle things in.

10.5.1.6 Be careful

In practice, it is very important to be careful when dealing with individual employees' issues and to maintain confidentiality at all times.

This is a minor matter. You want your employees to trust you as an individual and to feel like they can secretly share concerns. Once you break their trust, your working relationship effectively ends. Not only that, but once the word is read, your credibility will be confirmed.

10.5.1.7 Present well

We're not talking about your choice of clothing here. However, it is worth noting that your choice of clothing is in everyone's tone.

What we are referring to is the need to get up and address our team members. Strong communication skills are important, but you also need the ability - and confidence - to speak fully to your team.

You will be expected to give them instructions, give you training sessions and make these strange speeches. If you break into pieces in front of an audience, it is likely that it will be your delivery rather than the message of your presentation, which will become an important point of discussion.

10.5.1.8 Dealing (to tackle) with problems

If an employee encounters a problem with you, whether it be with their career, workload, office supplies, personal life or any other matter. You need to do your best to find a solution.

This is not always possible, but it is important that you recognize your team member's concerns and make a visible effort to address the issues.

Do not put things on the back burner, in the hope that they will separate themselves. This is especially important in the event of a dispute between team members. You need to deal with it quickly and decisively before the matter goes out of hand.

10.5.1.9 Help grow or Assist with Development

One of your roles as a manager is to foster career development opportunities for your employees and to support their professional aspirations.

This means training, coaching and practicing as appropriate and giving workers the opportunity to improve their skills. You have to make sure that they are aware of the opportunities available at home, allowing employees to work towards growth if they choose.

10.5.1.10 Provide effective cover

A typical GRAP employee is concerned with the level of cover provided by their manager on annual leave. GRAP is the abbreviation of "Generally Recognized Accounting Practice". If you are able to help them with their workload on certain days or on holidays, do so.

Whatever extra talent you have in your work day or within your team, it can be used to keep things ticking until the employee returns to work. When they see backups that come back in the first day, it helps to avoid major frustration and anxiety. It shows your care.

10.5.1.11 Provide occasional treatment

It may be something as simple as a piece of cake, a biscuit box, a fancy coffee shop or after-work drink, but it is always worth spending some of your hard earned money on your team members.

So, these are the terms which have to follow to win an Excellent Management support. One can easily make prominent himself by adopting these techniques in their professional & organizational way of life.

11
"Lean Six Sigma Implementation"

11.1 Introduction

Sigma's six principles use statistical and numerical methods to reduce the number of defects in the output. They emphasize the simplicity of the process, the quality of the parts and the logistics, and the responsibility of the employees to achieve the promised results.

Key Points to Implement a Project

There are some key points which are necessary for the implantation of project. Mandatory are as follow:

- Project
- Training

- Team
- Execute
- Plan
- Evaluate

11.1.1 Choose Project

The best way to implement the Six Sigma program is to start with a pilot project. You can identify a company process that is usually causing production problems or having other problems.

The process of identifying the pilot project involves the workforce involved and their input needs to be considered. Six Sigma only works when everyone is involved.

11.1.2 Training

The person who guides the implementation of the Six Sigma project should know six principles and principles of Sigma. In Six Sigma's terms, he should be a "black belt" expert.

In small businesses, a black belt is usually sufficient for a pilot project. A qualified new employee in the business can hire or train in the ranks. Training can be an overlap for Black Belt certification and pilot project implementation.

11.1.3 Team management

Once the company has chosen a Black Belt Team Leader, it has to assign team members who will assist in the process.

The company has to consult the workers involved in the pilot project. The team needs good staff, but also to run the Six Sigma Pilot Project after implementation.

11.1.4 Make plan

The team plans to implement it. The aim is to have an organizational structure that simplifies the production target preparation process to minimize defects.

Projects Manager (Black Belt holder) identifies areas of the problem, and workers at work assist with the solution. The project describes the steps the team has proposed to reduce team waste, increase worker efficiencies and eliminate barriers.

11.1.5 Execute

Six Sigma requires initial effort and then it is a continuous process. The pilot project will have to take preliminary steps and keep the organization in place for permanent application.

The team makes the necessary changes according to the plan and then wears a black belt to run it. The Green Belts support the new project and take on specific aspects.

11.1.6 Evaluate

Upon completion of the pilot project, an evaluation describes what worked and where the problems were encountered. The workers involved are a key source for diagnostic standards and parameters.

Assessment is the basis for permanent application in other areas of the Company's work. In a small business, the second round might include all the rest of the production activity.

11.2 Beneficial Tips

Without understanding what is being done and why, there will be very limited scope to improve Lean and Six Sigma. So, let's take a look at the top 10 tips for successful implementation of Lean and Six Sigma.

- Change in behavior

- Make Lean Six Sigma Compulsory
- Strong Platform
- Top-Down Approach
- High Profile Identification
- Right Measurement Systems
- Awareness of cultural Difference
- Having Communication Channels
- Perfect to start Lean Six Sigma (σ)
- Communities or Forums

11.2.1 Change of behavior

Industry experts believe that change of behavior is essential for effective implementation of change. This tendency in people is to work around it rather than to solve a problem, and this is where Lean and Six Sigma's willingness to permanently eliminate problems arising in the business process.

Even when people pledge to change their behavior, the tools will be added seamlessly. Training your manpower in Lean & Six Sigma is one thing, but without a change in attitude, the whole process will be educational only with no practical implications.

11.2.2 Make it Compulsory

Incorporating Lean & Six Sigma as part of the organization's goals and core strategy is one of the key components to its successful implementation.

And without it, the entire initiative will have a short-term life where people reject the process even before it is properly established in the organization.

Moreover, when an organization has a basic mechanism for the center of everything, combining lean and six sigma increases its chances of success.

11.2.3 Strong Platform

Businesses must have a strong platform or compelling reason to implement Lean and Six Sigma.

Strong platforms make a good impression on any customer. Which naturally inclines you towards it. A robust platform acts as a backbone for any organization.

11.2.4 Top-Down approach

Organizations around the world can apply Lean and Six Sigma to a bottom line. But industry experts believe that trying to involve senior and middle managers before ways to improve the process is worthwhile.

Their involvement in implementing Lean and Six Sigma towards improving key business processes will strengthen other affiliate practices that will also help increase adoption by others. Without the involvement of senior and middle managers, it is a difficult task to successfully adopt Lean and Six Sigma throughout the organization.

11.2.5 High Profile Identification

You need to choose projects that are endorsed by senior and middle management that passionately care about bringing people faster results.

This increases overall confidence in the lean and Six Sigma approach and will lead to widespread acceptance in the organization.

11.2.6 Right Measurement Systems

Organizations first need to understand that things that cannot be measured cannot be better.

With the proper measurement system in place, practitioners can decide on baseline performance and use data to make informed decisions. And when people understand the potential of lean and six-sigma, plans will quickly improve.

11.2.7 Awareness of Cultural Differences

Each organization has its own distinct culture, and experts believe that the culture is different between different geographical areas and different types of organizations such as local, corporate, small or medium, public, private and government.

It is better to avoid the assumptions about how you need to adopt lean and sigma and avoid the use of jargon unless this organization wants it. Doing so will facilitate the smooth implementation and integration of the lean and six sigma procedures between the two entities.

11.2.8 Having Communication Channels

Keeping open communication channels in an organization is an important aspect of timely completion of lean and six sigma projects.

On many occasions, addressing a small group or talking face-to-face to discuss important things is more effective than mass email communication.

11.2.9 Perfect to Start Lean Six Sigma

It is better to start with just a handful of people who will take over the leadership and responsibility of Lean and Six Sigma implementation and tell them that this will work for them, rather than just wasting their time and energy on skeptics or unbelievers. The word will spread positively through the networks of internal champions.

11.2.10 Communities or Forums

Knowledge management plays a key role in sustaining the growth or improvement of key business processes through lean and six sigma practices.

Lean and Six Sigma practitioners play an important role in knowledge management techniques to ensure learning from each other's experience, improving their capabilities with respect to the Lean and Six Sigma principles and tools regularly used in an organization.

11.3 Steps for Successful Implementation

There are 8 major steps in order to implement a successful project management. By following them, you can easily win a project management & can be applicable for a successful project implementation.

The steps are given below:

- Burning Platform
- Keep resources in the place
- Teaching
- Prioritize Activities
- Ownership
- Right Measurements
- Govern Programs
- Recognition

11.3.1 Burning Platform

To implement or think about lean or six sigma modes, we must have a burning platform. A burning platform can take many forms.

For example, some common or rare are like:

- We are experiencing huge quality losses and this accounts for more than 45% of our cost
- Our competitors are gaining 12% of our market share every quarter

By this, organizations are rarely motivated to implement continuous improvements to TPS (Lean) or Six Sigma or TQM or any improvement.

With the completion of this task, ever since Six Sigma became a visionary in the organization, everything else began to fall into place. So in order to increase organizational vision and value across our workforce, customers, partners and suppliers, we need to leverage our key leadership towards a common vision.

This ensures that the organization's environment is viable for change and capable of driving change, leveraging innovation and technology as key tools.

Finally, we need to take steps to achieve our vision. This ensures that we have visibility and strong support from the leadership. Leadership sponsors make sure we meet our organization's vision, thereby achieving excellence.

11.3.2 Keep resources in place

It is important to know what to look for in potential resources. Resources don't just help us succeed. We need to deploy them as a team, and this team must act as a change agent.

As an organization, we need to emphasize taking the initiative to empower the team, so we need domain expertise and knowledge. We also need to take care of our resources in terms of wages, and also have the resources to fit and realize the common vision.

11.3.3 Teaching Methodology

As the saying goes, "if I give a fish a man, he can survive only for one day. But if I teach this person to catch a fish, he can survive for lifetime".

Lean Six Sigma Organizations need to train their team members as powerful change agents in order to survive. Yellow Belt, Green Belt and Black

Belt training can help increase organizational awareness with skilled teachers. Employees identified for training should share the organization's vision.

11.3.4 Prioritize activities / Tasks

We need to know what to ignore and where to take the risk, and the question here is whether we can meet the key expectations of our organization's goals in terms of risk mitigation and expectation management.

Organizations should make it a top priority:

- Listen to the customer
- Identify quality standards by quality
- Ensure that the Lean Six Sigma efforts are aligned with business goals

11.3.5 Ownership

It is important to be clear who owns the Lean Six Sigma initiative. This includes setting up a committee to determine who is responsible for the entire team.

Ownership feels empowered and proud, and team members who are more committed, responsive and committed.

11.3.6 Right / Accurate measurements

What cannot be measured cannot be improved. By setting up a measurement system, practitioners can assess baseline performance and use data in objective decision-making and variable analysis. The key to measurement is to correct the right price.

11.3.7 Govern Programs (Making Reviews)

A proper governance structure can help maintain the momentum of a program. Poor governance or excessive governance can cause vision to fall apart.

For example, setting up a Business Quality Council (BQC) can help remove any obstacles that can slow the project down, and allow the project to follow timelines.

Appropriate governance also helps practitioners create a best practice sharing forum, which helps to redesign plans and highlights common challenges.

Without regular scheduled, fruitful meetings or review meetings, the program can halt courses and employees may lack guidance.

11.3.8 Recognition with Contributions

Rewards and recognition play a vital role in ensuring team members are satisfied with their role. They can help create excitement from the top to bottom and from the bottom up.

Rewards and recognition can also help drive innovation across the organization. Proper rewards and recognition ensure consistency in achieving excellent performance. Let me present my personal example of reward and recognition at the grassroots level.

12
"Benefits of Lean Six Sigma & Culture"

12.1 What Lean Six Sigma (σ) Culture?

Apparently, the biggest benefit Six Sigma has brought to the organizations that practice it is that it shifts employees from inactive participants to employees who often engage in these activities.

In order to create a culture of continuous sigma, the power of Six Sigma lies in changing the way we work through process change, as well as educating people on new ways to understand and solve problems.

Six Sigma Certification holders are accustomed to seeing themselves and their employees perform differently. They are taught to perform some specific task:

- View work in terms of process flow, not just departments and functions
- Involve yourself in your efforts to permanently improve
- Use the appropriate capabilities to create and implement solutions
- Take an active role in defining improvements and identifying solutions rather than relying on management

12.1.1 Importance of Culture

Once employees of Six Sigma have entered training and change is complete, organizations need a company culture that maintains these qualities and prevents employees from returning to their old behaviors and mentalities.

"Culture Eats Strategy for Breakfast."

12.2 Benefits of Lean Six Sigma Culture

Lean Six Sigma (σ) practices have been implemented by leading companies around the world, saving millions of dollars in many cases.

These guidelines and principles can be used by any business to improve and streamline internal processes and communications. Plus, these benefits aren't limited to just business.

Literally, any cost center can benefit from Lean Six Sigma provided there is commitment and purchase at all levels of the organization.

The key to understanding the benefits of Lean Six Sigma is to use and integrate highly trained people in the process, and those who have obtained the certification known as the Lean Six Sigma Black Belt.

The Lean Six Sigma Black Belt will have to undergo rigorous training in planning, development, project team management, measurement system analysis, organizational leadership and communication strategies to achieve its certification, which includes several levels.

When a company or organization goes ahead with putting these projects into practice, it will become increasingly more useful in its time and resource utilization.

There are some benefits of Lean Six Sigma Culture. Which are mentioned below:

- Increased Efficiency
- Better Customer Service
- Higher Quality Output
- Program Implementation
- A safer Workplace

12.2.1 Increased Efficiency

The main benefit of implementing the Lean Six Sigma culture for an organization is the increased efficiency at many levels. The Lean Six Sigma Master Black Belts are trained to analyze weaknesses in each workflow that can be reduced to achieve maximum performance in terms of time and resource allocation.

Lean Six Sigma integration can only be defined as a combination of its components, so each component needs to work to its full potential to achieve the most efficient results. Organizations that successfully implement Lean Six Sigma (σ) can expect to have the ability to increase measurement in both large and small processes.

12.2.2 Better Customer Service

By increasing the process performance and output quality, the Lean Six Sigma culture may have already acquired a part of the customer service formula.

However, aspects of the Lean Six Sigma process that focus on delivering better experience for the customer are also primarily focused on providing accurate hourly reporting, production schedules, bar coding, and time to meet customer needs.

12.2.3 Higher Quality Output

Moreover, to making the process more efficient, Lean Six Sigma programs also focus on achieving high quality at the same time. This is done by prioritizing work areas such as quality control standards and practices, inventory control, production schedules and literally eliminating quality issues in all operational processes.

By identifying current standards associated with these areas, proposing practical ways of improvement and making each employee master of those improvements, Lean Six Sigma's culture allows any organization to advance its products, processes, communications and services. Can help you achieve your goals.

12.2.4 Program Implementation

The implementation of the Lean Six Sigma program often represents a complete cultural change in the way an organization thinks and operates. There are several important aspects of the Lean Six Sigma culture that organizations must understand before setting up this program.

Lean Six Sigma programs are dynamic processes and require continuous and objective review of opportunities to improve them. Lean Six Sigma is a continuous cycle of process creation, process management and process improvement. The whole company should accept.

If this program is accepted with the full understanding of these points, any company can be successful in improving its performance, quality and customer service.

12.2.5 A safer workplace

Although probably not the most obvious benefit of successful implementation of the Lean Six Sigma, not to mention improvement across the board, only through the cultural affiliation and the nature of employee ownership which are integral components of the Lean Six Sigma integration, the net result is a significant as a safe workplace. Not only is it an advantage to refer to the team culture as mentioned above, it also goes to the right.

12.3 Benefits of Lean Six Sigma (σ) Methodology

The Six Sigma methodology provides a standard approach to problem solving in the case of ix Sigma projects.

To take advantage of the benefits or fruits of the Six Sigma method, the Six Sigma Yellow or Green or Black or Master Black Belt project should be launched. The main benefits of Lean Six Sigma are enlisted:

12.3.1 Reduce Operational Costs

Most companies believe that operational costs and risks are important factors. These factors contribute to lower profits or even losses.

Some risks cannot be eliminated, and operational costs are always high. The Six Sigma methodology can provide a road map that can be rapidly reduced to deal with the risks of an organization.

As well as make it more efficient and efficient for organizations to deliver its products or services. Difficult savings are the real reduction in dollars spent now. Reduced budgets, reduced staffing, reduced prices paid on purchase contracts, are just a few examples of difficult savings.

There is an estimated reduction in soft savings that should result from this project. Cost associated with supplying products and services with inefficient and ineffective standards. Six Sigma projects can be launched to reduce or reduce these costs are enlisted:

- Inspection Costs
- Rework Costs

12.3.1.1 Inspection Costs

A Six Sigma project can be created to minimize excessive inspection time or costs. In the case of such projects, the flow or process will be structured in such a way that any potential errors will be apprehended and where they occur in the process stage. Six Sigma is a quality assurance procedure.

12.3.1.2 Rework Costs

The term "Rework" refers to a "Re Work" that has already happened. Without a doubt, we can say that no user wants to bear this cost because the process has not met its first target.

The idea of rework means that the process is structured in such a way that incomplete or incorrect work is allowed to go further in the process so that it gets stuck in the flow and tries to correct someone.

Six Sigma schemes can be launched to create a fault mechanism or improve process detection. This is to reduce or minimize work in all operational operations. In other words, defect prevention should be the target of the Six Sigma project.

12.3.2 Customer Complaints

If the Six Sigma project aims to reduce consumer complaints, business units will be able to reduce the cost of consumer complaints to this organization. Customer complaints can greatly affect the bottom, especially.

Where there are significant errors in the product or service. Additionally; complaints can lead to the loss of business again from an existing client. The Six Sigma Project aims to improve customer satisfaction scores for a process, product or service.

12.3.3 Improve efficiency or Timeline

Six Sigma's projects help improve overall process performance. In addition, improving timelines in delivering process output or improving the timely delivery of products or services can become the focus of six Sigma projects.

To improve efficiency, Six Sigma projects can be used to reduce the number of machine setups or set-up hours in a manufacturing process, improve production or assembly lines production, wherever or manual interruptions in the functions that fully or partially automate the process.

12.3.4 Improve Accuracy, Controls & Policy Compliance

In this regard, Sigma's six projects help improve accuracy by reducing the defects-in-million-opportunities (DPMOs) in the value stream in the process. DPMO is the abbreviation of "Defects Per Million Opportunities".

The word "opportunity" means opportunity to make mistakes. DPMO is a possible measure of the error rate or ability of the business or manufacturing process. This measure considers both the actual defects and the number of possible defects at each opportunity.

As the DPMO increases, the sigma level process goes down and vice versa. The Sigma projector helps to measure baseline and target process accuracy in terms of DPMO and sigma levels.

This is a systematic way of measuring the accuracy of the process as it aims to prevent the presence of defects. According to Six Sigma's method, the process that is under statistical control is a stable process.

12.3.5 Improve Customer Service

The company's image is developed in large part through interaction with customers. Any company would like this interaction to be as stable as possible. The reason consumers are disappointed is oral criticism.

Six Sigma's projects can be launched to get to know users more fully, not just their problems or concerns. This approach can help businesses anticipate customer needs and address them through a systematic process.

Sigma's six plans help to assess the need to automate customer service functions. Six Sigma projects can be launched to address key customer service issues. It depends on the industry in which the company operates.

Sigma's six plans can help identify what changes are affecting customers, what is affecting the difference, and, ultimately, how to reduce the number of satisfied customers. Six such sigma projects also aim to improve customer and vendor satisfaction.

12.3.6 Improve flow of Cash

Six Sigma projects can also be targeted in relation to the business, which will improve DSO's day-to-day sales survival. DSO is the abbreviation of "Day Sales Outstanding".

If DSO is better, then cash flow is also better. The higher the DSO, the less the company's ability to convert credit sales into cash. Sigma's six plans are to reduce the variability of the invoicing process, accounts payable process, accounts receivable process, inventory management process, and more.

12.3.7 Improve Regularity Compliance

Generally, there are three aspects of regulatory compliance.

- Finance and Audit
- Information Technology
- Legal or by LAW

12.3.7.1 Finance and Audit

Under the umbrella of finance and audit, projects aim to improve the fund allocation process, reduce cycle time or turn round time in the cost estimation process.

12.3.7.2 Information Technology

In the area of information technology or information security, one project aims to reduce the risk of non-compliance, improve the quality of service of the help desk service.

12.3.7.3 Legal or by LAW

By law, the Six Sigma Project aims to improve the process of documenting and complying with critical, critical and unimportant documents.

13
"Criticism of Lean Six Sigma (σ)"

13.1 Why to not use it?

There are several reasons why you should not consider lean sigma in your business. Some are right. There are many misunderstandings. Still others are pure fiction. These are the ten most common reasons. These all things criticize the Lean Six Sigma (σ) approach. Which make it degrade, are given below:

- I've never heard about it
- It's just a fade
- Lake of Time
- Lake of Resources
- We're a small organization
- We're not manufacturers
- These are technical calculations
- Cheating with customers
- A poor experience
- A fear of unknown failure

13.1.1 I've never heard of a Six Sigma

That's definitely a good reason. Growing in popularity, Lean Six Sigma is still not part of the mainstream business. Which is one of the main reasons.

13.1.2 It's just a Fade

Lean Six Sigma is just attractive, like total quality management, theory of constraints and business process re-engineering.

Lean Six Sigma is different from other permanent improvement programs in three important ways:

- It has a laser-like focus on the customer
- Extensive use of data and analytics to make informed decisions
- The Return on Investment Trend, The Language of Management.

13.1.3 Pretended to be Lake of time / interest

We do not have time to devote to the official launch of the label Six Sigma. We're very busy setting you on fire.

13.1.4 Lake of Resources

Our business cannot afford the cost of implementing the Lean Sigma program. The short answer is that LAN Sigma programs do not necessarily require significant investment.

The point is that Lean Six Sigma (σ) should be seen as an investment. An investment that returns at least 5-10 times a year with the right projects.

13.1.5 Showing yourself as a small-scale organization

We're too small. Lean Six Sigma is for large organizations only. One of the most frequently heard comments from small and medium-sized business owners is "we hit the wall". This could mean inability to grow or grow a business with the same resources.

13.1.6 We're not a manufacturer

While lean sigma can be configured in manufacturing, the principles apply equally to the transaction and service environment.

In fact, the service industry is basically more wasteful than manufacturing because there is too much work and supply in the service "hidden".

13.1.7 It's is technical in calculations

Lean Six Sigma has a lot of statistics and advanced math. Most of our employees are front line operators. As all of them are not engineers.

Most organizations don't need statistics and advanced mathematics to enjoy the benefits of lean sigma. In fact, most principles and tools can be used by anyone quickly and easily.

Drawing a simple process map on a white board to identify spaces, redundancies, or obstacles in a process.

13.1.8 Cheating with Customer

Lean is a better fit for our business. We're going to start with the lean and then move to Six Sigma. By following this logic, you are deceiving your customers, your employees, your business, and yourself.

Lean & Six Sigma are not mutually exclusive and do not have to be applied in a linear manner. They complement each other. Being lean improves the speed and breadth of your business. It's about making business easier, doing more with less.

13.1.9 A poor Experience

We tried lean sigma years ago and didn't get good results. Ask yourself:

- Why didn't we have success?
- Did it matter to people, process or technology?
- What was the catalyst for joining this program?
- Was it running internally or through some key clients?
- Was leadership determined to make the program a success?
- If so, how was he committed?
- How is "success" defined?
- Were the goals and timetables realistic?
- Was it just about saving money or reducing headcount?
- Is the organization mature enough for this type of program?

These are some questions, which never free-up the mindset of a client. And always keep a deep effect of hanging or struck-ting on their minds.

13.1.10 A fear of an unknown Failure

Fear of the unknown or fear of failure. Of all the reasons listed, this is probably the most legitimate one. The problem is that very few people are willing to admit it or share it with others. Certainly pride is a factor.

But when you think about it, the fear of being unknown or of failure can paralyze. This prevents us from learning new skills, taking on leadership roles, or implementing programs such as Lean Sigma. To be innovative and thrive, fear has to be removed from the organization.

13.2 Criticisms of Lean Six Sigma (σ)
13.2.1 Lake of Originality

Coin sigma has been described as a "basic version of quality improvement", saying "there is nothing new. It includes something we used to call facilitators. They like different colored belts.

13.2.2 Inadequate / Insufficient for complex manufacturing

Six Sigma standards don't go far enough. Because every time consumers deserve a defective product.

For example, under the Six Sigma standards, seamless conductors are all defective, requiring flawless detection of millions of small circuits on the same chip.

13.2.3 Role of Consultants

The use of "black belts" as consultants has boosted the training and certification industry. Critics say a lot of the advice is to sell Sax Sigma through consulting firms, many of whom claim to specialize in Six Sigma when it comes to the tools and techniques involved or about these markets or industries.

13.2.4 Potential Negative Effects

Six Sigma is effective. But at what it is intended to do. It is simply designed to fix an existing process" & doesn't help to come up with new products or disruptive technologies.

13.2.5 Over-reliance on statistics tools

More directly critical is the "rigid" nature of Six Sigma, relying on methods and tools. In most cases, more attention is paid to reducing variability and finding any important factors, and less focus on creating robustness in the first place.

Depending on the importance of testing and the use of multiple regression techniques, the risk of statistical errors or commonly unknown types of errors increases.

One possible consequence of the Six Sigma array of P-value misunderstandings is the mistaken belief that the probability of a result of a mistake can be tested in any experiment without the evidence of external evidence or underlying mechanisms.

One of the most serious but most common misconceptions of abnormal statistics is to take a model that was developed by a research model building and subjected to similar data testing. Which are used to validate predefined models.

13.2.6 Stifling creativity in a research environment

Six Sigma is inappropriate in a research environment. "Excessive measurements & concentrations of Six Sigma is focused on reducing variability water down the discovery process.

Under Six Sigma, Under Six Sigma, the nature and nature of the discovery of a brain-storming & whole aspect of the discovery has been prevented.

13.2.7 Lack of systematic documentation

One last criticism, perhaps more in the literature of Six Sigma than in fiction, relates to the evidence of the success of Six Sigma. So far, documented case studies using Six Sigma's methods have been presented as the strongest evidence of its success.

Most cases are not documented either systemically or academically. In fact, the majority of the websites described are case studies, and, at best, outline. They do not mention the specific sigma methods used to solve the problem.

It has been argued that by relying on the Six Sigma standards, the management is burdened with the idea that something is being done about quality, while the resulting improvement is accidental.

13.3 Criticisms examples of Lean Six Sigma (σ)

Despite its scientific approach to quality improvement, there have been criticisms against Six Sigma. The sincerest is the theory that there is nothing new about Six Sigma because it imitates already existing and proven techniques.

To some extent, this argument has some credibility. But Six Sigma's supporters believe that as long as Six Sigma achieves more predictable results with very little effort, there is no problem in accepting and implementing it.

Despite criticism, all that Six Sigma does is apply concrete efforts to use existing methods in new ways.

Lean Six Sigma Green and Black Belt Training are often criticized. Good governance is about choice, so the decision to do nothing should be judged as much as the decision to do something.

When considering the decision to invest in Lean Six Sigma training, a sponsor organization needs to overcome the following.

- We do not prepare anything
- We've done it
- We are different
- We are very busy
- We have no money
- We have no processes!

- It will never work here, these terms Green Belt and Yellow Belt.
- Our actions are only "on demand"
- We are not broken; we do not need to be fix

Conclusions

- Lean is a waste removal technique by visualization while Lean Six Sigma is a waste removal technique by some statistical manners.
- Lean relies on 3 P's (Purpose, Process & People).
- There are some principles & phases of Lean Six Sigma that direct to an improved productivity. As, Lean & Lean Six Sigma interrelate in many ways. Similarly, they have many conflicts also.
- The foundation of Lean Six Sigma was developed in 1798 but the practical implementation was first done by TOYOTA in 1940's & 1980's.

- Lean Six Sigma is used to provide benefits to an organization in a profitable manner.
- Process mining is an automated, systematic way of defining an 'as is' phase of BPI to identify current workflows or process waste, obstacles, disagreements, and opportunities.
- There are 4 stages or phases by which a Process Mining helps to improves business process or to work for the betterment of Business Process Improvement (BPI)
- To increase or Boost the process cycle, DMAIC & DMADV are used.
- 7 principles of Lean Six Sigma help to increase efficiency & improved production.
- Some specific parts were introduced, which are using now to prevent defects & errors as well as their chances to be happen.
- There are 8 type of wastes exists within an organization are termed as, "D.O.W.N.T.I.M.E".

- D.O.W.N.T.I.M.E is the combination of "Defects, Over-production, Waiting, Non-Utilized talent, Transportation, Inventory, Motion & Extra-Processing."
- DMAIC is the abbreviation of "Define, Measure, Analyze, Improve & Control".
- DMADV is the abbreviation of "Define, Measure, Analyze, Design & Verify".
- A customer always has some hidden or unspeakable needs. Which often called voice of the client.
- The main thing is to understand your client's inner wishes or voice to get improved productivity.
- Lean Six Sigma's Certification is beneficial for both, Individuals & Organizations.
- The Certification has 5 levels generated as belts.
- The belts are of 5 colors with respect to their abilities & post.
- Belts are White Belt, Yellow Belt, Green Belt, Black Belt, Master Black Belt.

- Champion is not a belt, but a level. It is an initial level of Lean Six Sigma's Management.
- There are some key steps to adopt Improved Projects. By following them, an organization can get beneficial outputs.
- There are 5 Practical Strategies that direct an organization to get improved results.
- Identification of Improved Projects is much important thing or task to do.
- There are 5 step that make you able to identify Improved Projects for the efficient productivity.
- Management Support is a strategy. By attaining it, you can distinguish yourself as the top of the team.
- Management Support is the trust or the believe of your employees on you.
- There are 10 major steps to win Management Support. These are all about trust & Satisfaction of your clients.
- There are 6 key points. That are important to Implement an Improved Project.

- 10 beneficial tips can help you to form a strong Implementation platform.
- There are many benefits of Lean Six Sigma Methodology & its Culture.
- They help a lot in order to get 100% desired or accurate results as per client's requirements.
- They are much beneficial in attaining best efficiency, High Quality, Safe workplace, Low costs & many more.
- There are some reasons, why customers do no rely on Lean Six Sigma.
- There are some criticisms, that drop down the image of Lean Six Sigma in the market or organizational level.

The End

www.ingramcontent.com/pod-product-compliance
Lightning Source LLC
Chambersburg PA
CBHW060836220526
45466CB00003B/1122